T0010888

# The Jolly Bartender's GUIDE TO HOME BARTENDING

## NATHAN WILKINSON

PERMUTED
PRESS

A PERMUTED PRESS BOOK

The Jolly Bartender's Guide to Home Bartending
© 2023 by Nathan Wilkinson
All Rights Reserved

ISBN: 978-1-63758-560-3
ISBN (eBook): 978-1-63758-561-0

Cover art by Cody Corcoran
Interior design and composition by Greg Johnson, Textbook Perfect

**PERMUTED**
PRESS

**Permuted Press, LLC**
New York • Nashville
permutedpress.com

Published in the United States of America
1  2  3  4  5  6  7  8  9  10

*To my wife Meghan for encouraging me to write,*
*and for the many toasts we've shared.*

*Cheers!*

# CONTENTS

# WHO IS THE
# JOLLY BARTENDER?

I want to begin this book by dispelling a myth. You know, the idea that the Jolly Bartender is this guy that used to work at that bar in DC. Maybe he made you a drink or told you a joke. Happy guy, right?

The truth is, there is no *one* person known as the Jolly Bartender. The name I came up with had nothing to do with me, personally. It was all about the experience I had making cocktails at home. It was definitely more enjoyable and edifying than making them at work for someone else. So, I can say with confidence that the Jolly Bartender is you—anyone who wants to follow my adventure and make cocktails for themselves.

The idea for my website came a few weeks after I started posting photos of drinks on Tumblr, of all places. It was 2014. I was just starting out in my first gig at a McCormick & Schmick's, and I wanted to expand my bar knowledge beyond the menu items and the usual requests I got from guests.

The thing that took me from dabbling in a casual curiosity to a launching a crusade was a book I got on my twenty-first birthday. *The New York Bartender's Guide* (1997 edition) had been sitting on my shelf for seventeen years and got only occasional use. The recipes were packed several to a page with sparse instructions like "stir" or "shake" and a note about glassware. I didn't know at the time that fresh fruit juice was seldom used in bars—mixes being all the rage—but I found that I almost never went wrong if I followed the instructions. The book made me a better bartender, and I wanted to learn more.

Once I had a purpose for my blog, I only required a goal—something to keep me interested and challenge me in ways that working for tips never would. I decided to make and drink every recipe in that book. Eight years and two thousand cocktails later, I've more than met that goal; I've been witness to the rebirth of the cocktail, a trend that changed the bar scene in DC and across the world as restaurants lured guests with ever more complicated cocktail menus.

My daily challenge at work was figuring out how to make ever more outlandish and extravagant cocktails for paying guests. But while I was slinging Slings made with hand-squeezed cucumber water and roasted jalapeno syrup, I still kept coming back to the same idea— it doesn't have to be this difficult for it to be good. So, in my off time, I tried to stick to the basics: quality ingredients, proper glassware, and a handful of bar tools is all you need to start enjoying restaurant-quality drinking in your own home.

In 2020, the world changed again. Restaurants closed, mixologists were set adrift with nowhere to practice their skills, and servers found that the one job you could always count on as a backup in hard times wasn't a sure thing at all. The COVID-19 pandemic affected everyone connected to the restaurant industry, from the kitchen staff who started bottling cocktails to fill to-go drink orders to the guests who had to learn how to cook meals and make their favorite drinks at home.

The interest in home bartending is now stronger than ever, and would-be home bartenders have many choices of books to turn to for advice. The Jolly Bartender's Guide is here to help you stock and set up a bar and make mixing easy with tips I gleaned from professional bartending. Open the book and find that drink you always ordered when you went out. Learn how to master it. Then improve the recipe, name it, and make it your own. You are the Jolly Bartender in the bar you made yourself. What fabulous creations will you come up with next?

# DRINK RESPONSIBLY DISCLAIMER

If you've ever noticed the warning labels on liquor bottles or had one too many drinks at a bar, you are no doubt aware that there is danger in drinking excessively. Alcohol impairs our judgement and motor skills, meaning we are more likely to get hurt doing stupid things when we are drunk. And while some people hold their liquor better than others, no one is immune to the effects of alcohol. When you imbibe, make sure to never operate a motor vehicle or heavy machinery. Barring these dangerous decisions, use your judgement as to whether it's really a good idea to do a cartwheel, juggle knives, or engage in any intense activity after knocking back a few with friends. No one wants to end a fun night in an emergency room.

Fortunately, the risks of serious injury are somewhat reduced when we mix drinks in the safety of our own homes. There's no need to go anywhere, for one, so there should be no reason to drive impaired. And unlike a night of bar hopping, where there is compounded danger of over-indulging while making snap decisions about where to go next and how to get there in full view of strangers with dubious motives, you can control the environment to make sure you and your friends have a safe night.

That said, as the bartender in your home, it is now your responsibility to call a cab for your guests and cut someone off if it comes to that. You are in charge of safety as well as libations, and if you or any of your guests is hurt, you will undoubtedly share the blame. Such is the burden of being a host. Wherever possible, you should aim to be a mindful one.

But there are other concerns when deciding to build a home bar beyond the safety of your guests—one being the long-term effects on your health. With larger quantities of alcohol within reach, the temptation to drink too much or too often will always be there (take it from someone who drank all of the 1,500 cocktails in *The New York Bartender's Guide* in only three years). Having a home bar can lead to or exacerbate a drinking problem, so if you know you lack the self-control to have a bar in the home, maybe there are other, healthier activities you can pursue.

Lastly, you should consider family members' risks. If you have children—depending on their ages—you should store your bottles on high shelves or inside locking cabinets. Locks are a good investment if your household includes roommates or adult family members with a penchant for drinking; locking up your bar after use, just like the professionals do, protects your bar from theft and liability.

If, after this list of caveats, you still want to go ahead with plans to build a home bar, read ahead to find tips on stocking bottles and storing ingredients and purchasing glassware and tools. There are a lot of choices to make when you bring the bar experience home, but safety must come first. When it's your bar, it's your call; fun nights await, so long as safety is part of the plan.

# A NOTE ON THE ORGANIZATION & USE OF THIS BOOK

When I set out to put the Jolly Bartender website into book form, I wanted to take the most important information about my home bartending experience—the advice that was top of mind—and get it to anyone who wanted to start building a home bar. This is in no way a compendium of all the cocktails that have ever been made, nor even the thousands on my website. It's a guide from someone who has done it before and is in a position to offer advice.

Other books that cater to working bar staff include long lists of must-have liquors, glassware, and tools, as well as endless recipes for drinks no one has ever heard of, much less ordered. Since my readers don't have an unlimited budget and are most likely serving a limited clientele, I chose to address their most immediate questions: What do I need to have, and what recipes do I need to know? You have in your hand the answers to these questions about the craft of home bartending distilled down to the basic information. It's the tools, tricks, and ingredients that will set you up for a night of fun with your friends with no need to go out for drinks!

That said, the rest is up to you. You can dive deep into the sea of information and assemble a bar that is ready for any request, even those involving fresh-squeezed juice and specialized ice. But it is perfectly fine to loiter in the shallows, trying recipes and sticking to only the ones you like and are comfortable making. While that is true of any bartending book, I've taken steps to make both options convenient for fledgling home bartenders.

I've picked a handful of well-known cocktails that people love and organized the book around them, offering recipes that will appeal to their drinkers. No more flipping to a section of a recipe book with your favorite spirit and hoping to come across a recipe that sounds like something you'd like and that you also have the ingredients on hand to make. My chapters group similar recipes together with a master cocktail recipe. I suggest modifications and substitutions if you don't have all the ingredients, and I follow the master recipe with a list of variations. When appropriate, I group drinks by occasion if they share similarities. My hope is that each chapter will answer the question that the professional bartender asks every new guest: "Well, what do you usually like to drink?"

I also include questions and phrases often heard at bars in each chapter. There are no stupid questions. Hopefully my answers will satisfy your curiosity. There are plenty of well-researched books on cocktail history, a subject that is beyond the scope of this book and full of apocryphal stories that bar nerds trade at length. None of that will help you decide whether you should blend or shake a margarita. That is entirely up to you; the decisions about your home bar and your drink preferences are yours.

Finally, recognizing that creating and naming your own cocktails is an important component of having your own bar, I've included recipe cards where you can record your own inventions. Here's to many fun evenings shaking and stirring things up with friends. Cheers!

# DESIGNING & STOCKING YOUR OWN BAR

While I was working for tips, I talked with many curious guests about how a professional bartender might design a versatile bar at home that would satisfy their particular tastes as well as those of a variety of guests. The interest in building a home bar was there, but they didn't know where to begin: What liquors would they need to buy? How would they use the space in their home? What about glassware? I don't know how many of them took my advice, but I got the sense that the choices were overwhelming or the cost of doing it was too high. The mistake I saw them making over and over was they assumed that in order to make restaurant-quality drinks, they had to have a bar designed like the restaurant they loved.

Fortunately, that's not the case. A home bartender doesn't have to have twenty brands of vodka to fill every guest's request, nor do they typically care about using specially marketed glassware from the trendiest liqueurs. They don't need tools and containers designed for serving large numbers of guests. They don't even need a bartop or stools, though there is nothing wrong with having them. The point is, a home bartender gets to decide how the bar gets used and who they make drinks for. That takes a lot of pressure out of making decisions for your home bar.

Before going crazy and buying whole shelves of bottles from the liquor store, first consider how you will use the bar. Is it something you will use frequently for large parties, or is it just a luxury that you and a few close friends will get to experience? Will you display the decorative bottles on a shelf or keep your booze tucked out of sight in a plain cupboard? If you live in a small apartment, a tall bookshelf is a great way to store bottles vertically rather than take up a wide swath of wall space. For my bar, a small table in the corner of the dining space was all I needed to make almost any recipe, and that suited my purposes well.

## Tip on Shelf Height

Luxardo Maraschino liqueur comes in a bottle that is fourteen inches tall. It is the bartender's standard for the minimum space required between shelves. If a bottle of Luxardo Maraschino fits on the shelf, the chances are very good that every other bottle will fit as well. A top shelf (with nothing restricting bottle size above it) is a perfect place to store your Luxardo and those deluxe tequilas and vodkas whose bottles seem to get taller by the year.

# STOCKING LIQUOR

Once you know what your bar will look like and how it suits your tastes, I suggest you expand your liquor selection to include bases for recipes beyond what you and your friends enjoy already. I've seen many lavish bars built into basements complete with a back mirror, an ice bin, a beer chiller with taps, and a dozen stools. The sad thing is that this setup couldn't be used to make even one cocktail. A shelf of collectable whiskey you like to drink is not a functional bar unless your idea of a cocktail is whiskey and ice. Limiting your options like this is a simple mistake that I urge you not to make when stocking your home bar.

The list that follows is all the high proof liquors you will need to make every drink in this book. It is not an exhaustive list of every type of base spirit. Even so, don't feel as if you have to buy them all at once. There are a few must-have ingredients you should start with. Then, as you plan what recipes to make next, add a cordial or alpine spirit. I promise, you will be amazed at how one new bottle will lead you to the next as you try out recipes and become familiar with new flavors.

# Base Liquors

**Gin**—Gin is the original "blank canvas" of the classic cocktail base spirits. While gin is flavored with juniper and a long list of other botanicals infused during the distillation process, it is light tasting and easy to mix with. A London dry style gin is the most versatile, but if you prefer Old Tom gin or an American style of gin, by all means, get that as well as a London dry gin like Beefeater or Tanqueray.

**Brandy**—This spirit was once the mainstay of European hard liquors. Brandy is wine that is distilled and aged in oak barrels. Brandy, like whiskey, has regional differences. For that reason, I recommend home bartenders have one bottle of American brandy like Korbel or Christian Brothers and one bottle of French cognac like Rémy Martin or Hennessy. French cognac is spirit distilled from French white wine and aged in French oak. It notably softer than American brandy with a longer finish that is floral and fruity. The age statements on brandies are an alphabet of letters. For the beginning bartender, VSOP is a safe bet, denoting that the youngest cognac in the blend is at least four years old.

**Rum**—There are many types of rum, but few classic recipes call for spiced rum. Make sure you have at least one white (lightly aged) rum and one dark (well-aged) rum. White rums from Puerto Rico, like Bacardi, are the lightest in flavor. A dark Jamaican rum, like one from the Appleton Estate brand, will be heaviest on rich molasses flavor.

**Blended Whiskey**—Blended whiskies from Ireland, the United States, and Canada have a similar flavor profile and will not negatively affect a Tom Collins or daisy. These whiskies, while made from a variety of grains, are not malted or smoked. Their primary flavor is oak barrel aging and dried fruit notes. These will be your all-purpose mixing whiskies.

**Bourbon**—Unlike blended whiskey, straight bourbon comes from a single distillery and sometimes a single batch or barrel. Its signature flavor is vanilla, which comes from charring the oak barrels it is aged in. Bourbon can be more expensive when you seek rare bottles, but I'm a big fan of Evan Williams White Bottled-In-Bond and Jim Beam Black Label. Both are very traditional bourbons that will satisfy bourbon snobs and also make a great julep without requiring much of an investment.

**Rye**—Because of its larger portion of rye flour in its grain recipe, rye is a little spicier and more interesting than blended whiskies. It is essential for the classic Manhattan recipe and other stirred whiskey cocktails, where the base spirit takes center stage. One bottle of a brand like Rittenhouse or Old Overholt will satisfy this requirement.

**Scotch Whisky**—No other whiskeys taste like those from Scotland. (In the United States and Ireland, the typical spelling is "whiskey," while the Scotch and Canadians prefer spelling it "whisky.") While all scotches differ from each other, they generally have a sweet, malted barley note and a whiff of peat smoke on the nose. I recommend getting one bottle of blended scotch like Dewar's, Grant's, Teacher's, or Chivas Regal. These will be your mixing scotches that actually taste better when diluted with soda and fruit juices. If you are a single malt fan, be sure to have one of your favorites on the bar as well. I often mix with a smoky single malt scotch like Laphroaig when smoke and peat are important components to a cocktail's profile. If you don't know much about single malt whisky but are open to trying it, it never hurts to pick up a bottle for your home bar. Even if you don't enjoy it, someone will appreciate that you have it. Remember, there are no bad single malt scotches, but the best are the ones you will drink. Find your own.

**Tequila**—All tequila is made from blue agave plants grown in Jalisco, Mexico. They all share similar peppery, herbal, and fruity notes. That said, there is a lot of bad tasting tequila out there, and you'll want to avoid buying too cheaply. A fifth of tequila should cost you about twenty bucks at the very bottom of the price range. You will want to get one white (blanco) tequila and one aged/gold tequila (reposado or añejo) because their tastes vary enough to be suited to different recipes. When it comes to fair quality tequilas for the price, look for Sauza or El Jimador for white and gold varieties. Milagro, Don Julio, and Patrón are good quality tequilas, while Corralejo will be worth its place on your top shelf (see tip on shelf height).

**Vodka**—It seems strange to mention vodka last, like an afterthought, but vodka is a newcomer in the world of classic cocktails. That is why old cocktail books will specify gin for martinis and daisies. Though nowadays we can't imagine making cosmopolitans without the clean taste of vodka. When stocking your bar with vodka, you really only need one bottle of your favorite brand, be it Smirnoff, Grey Goose, or Tito's. If you can't live without marshmallow or birthday cake flavored vodka, get that as well—those flavors can't be replicated at home, so no judgement here. But it is important to remember that you can flavor your own vodka by steeping fruits and berries in a jar for up to two weeks. That means it's pretty much unnecessary to have a dozen bottles of flavored vodka unless you want to.

# Cordials & Flavorful Liqueurs

**Where to shop:** liquor store/specialty wine shops
**What to buy:** St-Germain, Luxardo Maraschino Liqueur, Amaretto, Bénédictine, génépy, or Chartreuse

**Crèmes**—this is a category of sugary spirits that are essential to getting strong flavors into your cocktails. While there are more than a dozen crème flavors, you should really narrow your purchases to the following: crème de cassis (black currant), crème de menthe (mint), crème de cacao (chocolate), crème de violette (violet), crème de banane (banana), and crème de noyaux (almond). Some crèmes come in different colors, crème de menthe, for example, comes in green and white (clear), while cacao comes in dark (brown) or white (clear). Use your own judgement when selecting these based on your preferences. While clear spirits have no artificial dye in them and may be more versatile in cocktails, some drinks benefit from the bright colors, such as that green crème de menthe and the pink shade of crème de noyaux. When it comes to trusted brands, I avoid Bols, but that is a personal preference. Leroux and DeKuyper are reliably good and Tempus Fugit makes a top shelf series of crèmes that are worth every penny for their notably fresh taste.

**Flavored Brandies**—like crèmes, flavored brandies are very sweet ingredients that provide a cooked fruit—rather than fresh fruit—flavor. They have a brandy base and contain artificial colors and flavors. Use them sparingly to balance a cocktail and add sweetness. The key flavors to focus on here are apricot, blackberry, and cherry brandy because they make excellent dessert cocktails and cobblers. Jacquin's is an easy-to-source brand for these flavors and you should get one of each eventually. Cherry Heering is a deluxe black cherry brandy that will really class up your flavored brandy collection.

One absolute must-have item from this category is triple sec, a bitter orange spirit used in margaritas and a number of refreshing cocktails. Most triple sec is not made from a brandy base; instead, distillers choose a distillate of beet root for its clean flavor. While there are many budget triple sec brands out there, I'd urge new home bartenders to invest in Cointreau or Pierre Ferrand's Dry Curaçao. Bottled at higher proof, these orange spirits really sparkle in the glass. For richer, aged orange brandy-based spirits, look to the well-known Grand Marnier brand but don't pass up Royal Combier if you happen upon it. Both will serve you well.

Some flavored brandies are known as proprietary spirits. They are often higher proof and a little less sweet. Many contain more than one signature flavor and are often made with a secret recipe of ingredients that is well guarded by the distiller. These include St-Germain (elderflower liqueur), Chambord (black raspberry liqueur), Luxardo (maraschino liqueur), Frangelico (hazelnut liqueur), Tuaca (vanilla and citrus liquor), and Mandarine Napoléon (mandarin orange liqueur). Of the above mentioned, only St-Germain and Luxardo Maraschino are absolute must-haves on a modern bar, and it is certain that one of your guests will request them at some point. Domaine de Canton is a ginger flavored brandy by the makers of St-Germain. Its uses are somewhat limited, but it does make an appearance in one recipe in this book, so consider it or an off-brand ginger brandy as an impulse purchase.

**Amaretto**—This intriguing after dinner cordial doesn't just taste like almonds. If it did, crème de noyaux would take its place. Amaretto is actually made from the Saronno cookie, a very particular baked good that takes its name from the Italian town where they are famously baked. There are a lot of brands of amaretto coming from this part of Italy with Disaronno being the most famous. Check out Luxardo

Amaretto as well as Lazzaroni, each with their own unique combination of flavors.

**Alpine Spirits**—This is a rather loose category of strong spirits from France, Germany, Italy, and other mountainous regions of Europe that are characterized by their overwhelmingly complex fruit and herbal flavors. Principal in this group are the green and yellow Chartreuse liqueurs used in The Last Word and other sidecar variations. These spirits are so unique and their recipes so well protected, there is nothing else like them in the world. They are pricy, however, so put one or both of these on your wish list to add to your bar after your initial investment.

Less expensive but no less mind-blowing is génépy. This is a generic word for alpine spirits like Chartreuse made by several European distillers of which Dolin is one. Having a génépy on your bar is not critical, but be on the lookout for them at specialty wine stores that sell spirits.

**Strega**—This is a brilliantly golden Italian Alpine spirit flavored with mint and citrus flavors. It mixes especially well with bourbon and citrus juices but does not figure too prominently in the cocktail canon. For this reason, it's not an essential unless it becomes one of your favorites.

**Bénédictine**—This is not a true Alpine spirit because it is not from the mountainous region of France. But Bénédictine deserves mention because it is in many classic cocktails like the Monte Carlo and Bobby Burns. Bénédictine came along after Chartreuse and benefited from modern advertising campaigns that introduced dozens of recipes, of which this book contains only a few. Nevertheless, you should get a bottle when you get the chance.

# Vermouth & Fortified Wine

**Where to buy:** specialty wine shops or grocery stores
**What to buy:** one French (dry) and one Italian (sweet) vermouth,
Harveys Bristol Cream sherry, and Sandeman ruby port

**Vermouth**—At one time, drinking a glass of vermouth was as common as having a glass of wine. That shouldn't be surprising since vermouth is simply wine that has been flavored with herbs, barks, seeds, and spices. The two vermouths every bar requires are the French (dry) and Italian (sweet) varieties. For the dry, look for brands like Dolin and Noilly Prat to class up your martinis. Sweet vermouth used in Manhattans can be mild, like Martini & Rossi Rosso, or you can look to more bitter Italian vermouths like Carpano Antica Formula or Cocchi di Torino to add depth to your Negronis.

**Sherry**—Sherry is a fortified wine from Spain. It is usually consumed at room temperature in mild climates (not warm), but it has many applications in cocktails. A cream sherry like Harveys Bristol Cream is a good starting point for a home bar. With this, you can make Sherry Eggnog and several dessert cocktails. It is also fun to experiment mixing cream sherry with bourbon and scotch in proportions similar to a Manhattan for a rich winter treat. Lighter sherry cocktails like the Carmen Cavallaro require the Manzanilla or Fino types of sherry that are fruity with a nutty finish. Like most wines and spirits, sherry is an acquired taste. You should figure out if sherry is your thing before expanding your collection.

## A Note on Storing Vermouth & Fortified Wines

The higher alcohol content of vermouth and fortified wines protects it from turning sour as quickly as a bottle of wine. However, vermouth does tend to lose its flavor over time if it is not kept chilled and vacuum sealed. One way to prolong your vermouths flavor is to buy smaller bottles, if you don't intend to drink them very quickly. A small bottle will have less space for oxygen to make contact with the wine. It is this oxidation that you want to avoid; so, if you do buy a large bottle of Carpano Antica (some merchants only carry the one-liter size bottle), have a plan for how you will store it after it is opened.

**Port (or Porto)**—Port is a type of dessert wine that retains the sweetness of its residual sugar by being fortified before it is fully fermented. Porto refers to fortified wine from Portugal, while port is the generic term for the style and can be made in any country. Port comes in ruby and tawny varieties, the tawny describing the faded red color of an extended aging process. While tawny port is wonderful by itself, the extra aging comes with a higher price tag. Most cocktail recipes that call for port require ruby port for its gem-like red luster that brightens cocktails and makes flips and fizzes a lovely pink. Sandeman Ruby Porto is my personal recommendation for the home bar, but don't feel like it is absolutely necessary to get. Consider picking up a bottle during the winter holidays.

# Beer & Wine

**Where to buy:** grocery store, specialty wine store,
drug store, or corner store
**What to buy:** dry white wine, bold red wine, champagne
or sparkling wine, pilsner-style lager, and stout

I like to have several varietals of wine and styles of beer on hand for my own enjoyment or as a simple beverage to offer a friend. These are familiar and easy go-to options for the guest who doesn't like a mixed drink. There are, however, a few cocktails made with beer and wine that are available to you if you have the right ingredients.

**Beer**—One's beer choice is truly their own these days. There are so many styles of beer to choose from at the store, and if you keep chilled beer in your refrigerator for your own enjoyment, by all means, stock what you like to drink. There are some cocktails like the Michelada that require a lager beer, while stout or malty dark beer can be used in some dessert cocktails. Having one of these styles will be handy.

**Wine**—For the purposes of mixing, an inexpensive dry white wine and a bold red wine are not required but have their uses in some cocktails. Don't spend too much on these, though. An inexpensive sauvignon blanc and merlot will probably suffice. You can't as easily get cheap champagne for a French 75, but sparkling wine is acceptable as long as it is dry. Because sparkling wine loses its fizz quickly after it is opened, consider getting small bottles or single-serving sizes in bottles or cans.

# Amari & Aperitivos

**Where to buy:** liquor stores and specialty wine shops

**Amari**—An amaro is an Italian wine-based spirit flavored with citrus peels and bitter herbs and barks. They are usually taken neat at room temperature to help settle the stomach. Amari have gained popularity in recent years because of their distinct bitterness and low alcohol content, which means drinkers can enjoy big flavors in moderation without the intoxicating effect of drinks like a Manhattan or martini.

It's not a requirement for a home bar to have a collection of amari, but consider getting one to mix with. The following are a short list of my favorites in no particular order. They all have mildly bitter notes of citrus peel and spice.

- Amaro Meletti
- Montenegro
- Amaro Averna
- Ramazzotti
- Amaro Nonino
- Luxardo Amaro Abano

**Aperitivos**—Aperitivos, on the other hand, are spirit-based bitter liquors. Slightly stronger than amari, these appetizer spirits are—as their name suggests—good for stimulating the appetite before dinner. Among the most important for a home bartender to get to know are the extremely bitter Campari, the milder Aperol, and the intense and soothing Cynar. The varieties and styles of cocktails that these bitter liquors open up to your bar is invaluable, so I encourage you to start with one of these. Manhattan fans will gravitate to Cynar, while a Negroni fan already loves Campari. If you are not sure if you like aperitivos, get Aperol. You won't be sorry.

# Anise Flavored Spirits

**Where to buy:** liquor store
**What to buy:** one of the following: Pernod, Ricard,
or an absinthe of your choice

**Absinthe**—This French spirit was all the rage in the 1800s. It had a prominent anise flavor and bitterness that made it best consumed mixed with water and sugar. Absinthe, unfortunately, obtained a bad reputation around the world for its intoxicating effects—due more to its high alcohol content than its wormwood botanical. While the end of prohibition brought back most liquors, absinthe remained banned until relatively recently. The absinthe found in liquor stores today are no different from those of the past; they still have the wormwood botanical and will be among the highest-proof bottles you have on your bar. Absente Absinthe Refined is the leading brand of absinthe available worldwide and local distillers are taking a crack at it as well. You may not be a fan of absinthe, but you can't make a Sazerac without it, so pick up a bottle (you can get Absente Absinthe Refined in 8 oz. bottles) or one of the substitutes below.

**Pernod and Ricard**—These came into vogue following the banning of absinthe. They fit the category of liqueurs, but they are not Alpine or fruit brandies. Both typify French café drinks straight from the bottle, as if you are enjoying absinthe with the sugar and water added for you. These substitutes are readily available where absinthe is harder to find and will make your Sazerac just as special as absinthe.

# Bitters

Where to buy: liquor store
**What to buy:** one or two aromatic bitters,
one orange bitters, and a lifting bitters of your choice

Bitters are the finishing touch for spirits-forward cocktails like the old-fashioned and Manhattan. They also introduce spicy or fruity complexity to juicy and tropical drinks. For these reasons, you can't ignore the importance of having a few bottles of bitters on hand for certain occasions. Bitters come in two categories: binding bitters and lifting bitters.

**Binding Bitters**—Binding bitters do exactly what you would expect of them; they help unify the flavors of spirits in strong cocktails. An old-fashioned without binding bitters would taste like a disappointing combination of whiskey and sugar. It is the bitters that add spice and scent that give the old-fashioned traction—the experience of a lingering flavor on your tongue that lasts long after you have swallowed a sip. While there are many brands of binding bitters, the two most important are Angostura bitters and Peychaud's Bitters. Angostura makes a tropical spice and bark bitters that goes as well with classic whiskey drinks as it does in punches, while Peychaud's has a fruitier and more herbal scent that is essential to the Sazerac cocktail. Beyond these two main brands, look for any bitters labeled "aromatic" from brands like Bitter Truth, Fee Brothers, Hella, or Bittermens.

**Lifting Bitters**—These bitters have light, fruity, or herbal scents that change the flavor profile of a cocktail. They tantalize the senses and bring different flavors forward, much like the addition of a cordial or liqueur. Grapefruit or lemon bitters can "lift" the scent of citrus peel to your nose when you sip a sidecar. Celery or hellfire bitters can add a savory touch and heat to a Bloody Mary or tequila cocktail. Lifting bitters are fun to experiment with, but less important to most cocktail recipes than binding bitters with one exception. Orange bitters are used in almost as many recipes as aromatic bitters, mainly because they function as a binding ingredient. If you only buy one lifting bitter, it should be orange. For a purely orange zest flavor, get Regan's orange bitters. Other orange bitters have more of a baking spice profile: Angostura orange bitters, Fee Brothers, and Hella are best put to use in Manhattans and old-fashioneds.

# Fruit Brandy
# & Other Non-Essentials

**Where to buy:** liquor store
**What to buy:** possibly one apple or grape spirit
to make a sidecar or pisco sour

Fruit brandy, as opposed to fruit flavored brandy, is a spirit made from fermented fruit juices. These spirits don't taste like the fruits from which they are made and they have very little sugar content. For this reason they make excellent base spirits when mixed with juices and sodas, but shouldn't be treated like a flavoring ingredient as one would a flavored brandy. These spirits have no artificial colors like flavored brandies and are usually more expensive to produce and purchase than flavored brandies.

If you have purchased the recommended bottles up to this point, you have all the spirits you need to make the master recipes in this book. Some variations of these cocktails will be out of reach, however, without one or more spirits made from distilling fruit juices. The following is a list of non-essential spirits that will allow you to cover every recipe in the book.

**Applejack, Apple Brandy, and Calvados**—These are all brandies distilled from apple cider. Applejack or apple brandy are important in variations on the sidecar and daisy and shouldn't be overlooked. Laird's Applejack 86 hits the sweet spot at the best quality for the lowest price. Calvados is the deluxe apple brandy from the Normandy region of France. Think of it as the Cognac of the apple brandy world. Of course, though any sidecar or sour variation will be improved with Calvados, its higher price and quality (its terroir) make it more suited to enjoying neat from a snifter.

**Pisco, grappa, and singani**—These are all white grape spirits that have a distinctive floral note. While Chilean piscos tend to be smooth and sometimes lightly aged, Peruvian pisco, Italian grappa, and Bolivian singani have more character. I mention this spirit category mainly to point out that a pisco sour is one of the best sour drinks ever, and it would be a shame if you couldn't pull it off. So, while these grape spirits are not essential to your bar, you will really benefit from picking one up, if only for this cocktail.

**Slivovitz and kirschwasser**—These two and other fruit brandy types are fun to experiment with but are not core ingredients in this book. Slivovitz is a type of plum brandy originating from Eastern Europe. It is strong with a floral nose and alcoholic bite. Kirschwasser is a German cherry brandy that is strong and smells vaguely of black cherries. It appears in several places in this book's variations on classics.

There are also numerous fruit brandies out there—as many as there are fruits, as it turns out. Small distillers are making peach, pear, cherry, apricot, and plum brandies (like Rakia, if you are into plum brandy from Eastern Europe). Unlike flavored brandies, distilled fruit juice brandies don't taste like the fruit they come from, just as brandy doesn't taste like wine and whiskey doesn't taste like barley. While it is nice to slip a nip of kirschwasser into a Manhattan or float pear brandy on a sidecar, these fruit brandies are not a requirement for a basic home bar. Pick them up if you find them, and use them to become a more versatile bartender, but most of these are not a priority for your bar.

**Akvavit or aquavit**—A Scandinavian caraway spirit that is savory and delicious, designed to go with pickles and salted meats served on the smorgasbord. It also makes kick-butt sours and martinis and can enhance a Bloody Mary. Scandinavian people often make their own akvavit by steeping whole caraway and other seeds in vodka for a few days, but Linie Aquavit and Aalborg Akvavit can be found in the US if you want to try these delicacies. Check out the Appendix for a home-made akvavit recipe that is as good as the bottles you find in stores.

# Fresh Ingredients & Mixers

**Where to buy:** grocery store, supermarket, or convenience store
**What to buy:** fresh citrus and berries, herbs, cans of pineapple juice, cranberry juice, tomato juice, club soda or sparkling water, tonic, ginger beer, and cola; Tabasco sauce, horseradish sauce, and Worcestershire sauce; grenadine, honey, and crème of coconut; half-and-half or cream

Whether your bar is in your living room, basement, or some other part of your living space, it's a good idea to have a refrigerator close by for citrus and herbs, as well as for chilling your wine and beer. That may mean you need a cube fridge under the bartop or easy access to a freezer where you make ice. Ample pantry storage for cans of mixers and juices is also helpful.

**Citrus**—Keep fresh lemons, limes, oranges, and the occasional grapefruit refrigerated. They will last about a week and a half and provide fresh squeezed juice as well as citrus wheels and zests for garnishes.

**Herbs**—Mint for mojitos and juleps has to be fresh, but it will only last a few days in the refrigerator. The same goes for rosemary, dill, and celery for Bloody Mary garnishes. Consider only stocking these in advance of a party where herbs will be a major feature, such as mint on Derby Day. Ideally, growing herbs in your own garden would ensure a constant supply.

**Juices and Sodas**—Some juices are better stocked in cans, ready to open when called for. These are tomato, pineapple, and cranberry juice, among others. Chilling these makes it easier to serve cold drinks with less dilution due to ice melting. It is also important to have chilled sodas like ginger beer, tonic, and cola, as well as club soda or sparkling water. If you prefer a soda machine, by all means use it, but beware—some water sources like wells impart a distracting or unpleasant taste to soda water and ice. If you insist on using a soda machine like Soda Stream, filter your water before serving it.

**Syrups and Fruits**—The two most commonly used cocktail sweeteners are simple syrup, which I encourage bartenders to make, and grenadine, which is easiest to buy. Rose's Grenadine is the most widely available. It's basically pomegranate-flavored corn syrup, but it is shelf stable, whereas the brands that use fresh pomegranate juice spoil after you open the bottle.

Some recipes in this book call for raspberry or pineapple syrup, both of which are easy to make at home (see the Appendix on syrups and infusions). Obviously, it is prudent to buy the fruit and make and cool the syrup prior to having guests over. But a helpful hint with syrups is that you can make a syrup from any fruit or fruit juice you have left over from making drinks. That means that unused garnishes like strawberries and open cans of apple juice or pineapple juice can be preserved by cooking them into a sugary syrup.

Other alternatives to simple syrup include maple, honey (mixed with equal parts water), and agave syrup. There is an occasional recipe calling for orgeat, which is an almond syrup that was once hard to find but is now in most supermarkets and wine shops. These alternative sweeteners can really alter a cocktail's flavor and add a touch of the exotic to everyday recipes.

# Bar Tools & Glassware

If you've followed my recommendations for stocking your bar, you should now have between twenty-five to thirty bottles of liquor, including vermouth and fortified wine. This is a small but very versatile collection of spirits you can use to make almost every recipe in this book. Now you need the tools to make the drinks and glassware to serve them in.

## Bar Tools

**Where to buy:** department store or kitchen supply store
**What to buy:** mixing glass, measuring container, bar spoon, shaker tin, strainer, cone strainer, peeling tool, citrus zest tool, muddler, citrus juicer, Lewis bag, blender, ice cube trays, and molds

Restaurants often equip their bar staff with a plethora of tools, some essential and some extraneous. For your home bar, the list of necessary tools is pretty short assuming you already have a functioning kitchen. Mixing glasses, spoons, and peeling tools can be repurposed from your kitchen, and blenders and strainers serve a dual purpose of preparing food as well as making cocktails. But there are a handful of bar-specific tools that will make mixing easier. Below I address the items you will need to make all the recipes in this book.

**Mixing glass**—A mixing glass is a clear (preferably glass) container for stirring cocktails on ice. To be useful, it needs to be wide enough to swirl ice with a long bar spoon, but deep enough to contain one or more cocktails. It should also be dishwasher safe and tempered to withstand rapid changes in temperature so that it doesn't crack. A pint glass from your bar glassware shelf will do nicely because it meets all the above requirements. It is, however, nice to have a pouring spout on one side to make pouring easier. Decorative mixing glasses like

Barcraft's Yarai glasses are a nice touch when it comes to showing off to your guests. These are less expensive than you'd expect and can be found in the kitchen section of most department stores.

**Bar spoon**—While it's not a requirement, a bar spoon with a long, slender handle and small head looks better than a knife or chopstick when you are stirring someone's drink. Look for the spiral-shaft spoons that allow the spoon to rotate in your fingers as it moves along the edge of the mixing glass.

**Measuring spoon set**—Some measurements will be too small to eyeball in your jigger, and you really don't want to get the wrong measurement for an ingredient like chili powder. A set of measuring spoons from your kitchen will help with measuring dry ingredients and small quantities of liquids like bitters.

**Strainer**—Two types of strainers are common in restaurants: the Hawthorne and julep. The julep strainer is a relic of the days before straws were in common use. In the heyday of mint juleps, guests were offered the julep strainer—a short-handled, glass-width scoop with widely dispersed holes. They used this strainer to hold back the crushed ice in the julep cup while they drank the liquid. Just as the julep cup is a specific vessel for serving a mint julep, a julep strainer is an accessory that the drinker uses. It's not a bartender's tool. While you can attempt to use a julep strainer to strain a cocktail from your shaker or mixing glass, it's a clumsy tool for the job. Ice bypasses the edges that don't completely cover the top of your mixing vessel and liquid pours slowly through the holes. In modern restaurants you often see a julep strainer in the bottom of a bar sink, straining muddled mint and fruit before it clogs the drain. If you want to make mint juleps, serve them with a straw and avoid an unnecessary piece of bar equipment.

For making cocktails at home, the Hawthorne is the only strainer you will need. These have a spring edge to hold the strainer in place on your mixing glass when you pour, giving you better control. The Hawthorne has the advantage over julep strainers because it has two types of straining action. You can press the strainer down on the mixing glass and completely strain ice chunks from the drink you are pouring. You can also allow smaller pieces of crushed ice to pass through the spring by sliding the strainer back so that the pouring edge is only strained by the spring. This technique is very useful on slushy drinks where you only want to remove large ice pieces or muddled ingredients from the drink you are pouring.

**Cone strainer**—a fine mesh strainer is used over a cocktail glass to catch tiny shards of ice or muddled ingredients you don't want floating on top of drinks you serve. The mesh strainer is also useful for removing solids from fruit syrups you might cook in the kitchen. You will get a lot of use out of a cone strainer for both your bar and your kitchen. When a recipe requires a cocktail to be double strained, it means to strain through a Hawthorne strainer and a cone strainer at the same time.

**Shaker tin**—If you've seen bartenders at restaurants using a tin that fits over a pint glass to shake drinks, you might assume you need something like that for your bar. In fact, these shakers, known as Boston shakers, are great for making several drinks at once, but they are impractical and a little heavy for home bartending. They have a further drawback of being messy, as they sometimes pop open when not sealed correctly and leak everywhere during a vigorous shake. That's not something most home bartenders want happening in their houses.

At home, a mixologist can take the time to be tidy and precise. The shaker that does this for me is a cobbler shaker. These come as sets of three parts: a base, a lid with a built-in strainer, and a cap that can be removed for easy pouring. This strainer works equally well with a Hawthorne strainer and can even double as a mixing glass. The cobbler shaker is small enough to fit in one hand but can hold two cocktails worth of liquid. Having two cobbler shakers allows you to impressively shake with both hands. The built-in strainer is an added benefit that other shakers don't have. It adds froth to egg white cocktails by aerating the mixture to make your whiskey sours even fluffier. Double straining from a cobbler shaker through a cone strainer also removes fruit pulp from daiquiris and sidecars. It's really a win-win-win shaker for the home bartender.

The one drawback bartenders cite with the cobbler shakers is that the cap can be hard to remove after a vigorous shake with ice because the chilled contents create a vacuum seal. That's not a huge drawback if you aren't working in a high-volume bar. This problem is negated in the Japanese-style cobbler shakers that have taller caps with beveled edges that you can lift with your fingers to release the vacuum. If you already have a Boston shaker and it works for you, I'm not suggesting you get a cobbler shaker. You will scratch your pint glasses with the Boston, though, and I'd prefer to use those to serve beer.

**Measuring container**—The jigger is the main measuring container for bartenders. It's a double-sided, hourglass-shaped tool designed for ease of use in a busy bar. The best ones have interior lines for $\frac{1}{4}$ oz., $\frac{1}{3}$ oz., 1 oz., and $1\frac{1}{2}$ oz. measurements because these are the typical portions that most recipes require. My recommendation for the best jigger is the OXO brand. These have a rubber grip between the cups and are made of a single piece of aluminum. I've had so many of the cheap fused aluminum jiggers break in half when they are dropped. You get what you pay for in tools, and a poor-quality jigger just won't last very long.

## A Brief Note on Shaking

How long or vigorously do you need to shake? That depends on the type of drink you are making and your personal preference. A quick rule of thumb is fifteen rapid shakes with the shaker held horizontally and supported on the bottom and top with each hand. This ensures a good amount of chilling (the outside of the shaker tin should frost over slightly), and a desirable amount of dilution for juicy cocktails like a margarita. Of course, this requires physical effort on the part of the bartender. Guests find it irritating when the bartender halfheartedly tips the shaker from side to side while talking to someone. Making a drink well means a strong shake.

The personal preference aspect of shaking comes up when shaking a cocktail with no juice, like a martini. There's less liquid and it won't require very many shakes to get cold. Shaking more than ten times just adds more ice chips and dilution, which may or may not be your guest's preference. Consider what the outcome of the shake will be for your cocktail when determining how long to shake.

Drinks with egg whites or whole eggs need the longest and most vigorous shaking to create foam. These often require fifteen shakes with no ice (dry shake) first and a second round of fifteen shakes (a wet shake) with ice for chilling. If you are making a flip, which has a smaller volume than a fizz, you should do fifteen shakes dry and fifteen shakes wet. This way the foam will be tall with minimal dilution from melting ice. Fizzes always require at least two shakes and the shake with ice should be at least thirty to maintain the foam but also chill the larger amount of liquid which may include cream and juices.

Of course, you can use any measuring container you like, be it a graduated shot glass or a small measuring cup with a pour spout. You don't need shiny Japanese jiggers that require a lot of bartending dexterity to use. Being comfortable with your tools is more important than how they look.

**Peeling tool**—I use a simple potato peeler for my home bar. I like the ones with a single hand grip for making twists because they give you leverage against the fruit you hold in the opposite hand. Fancy broadbladed peelers are really for completely removing potato peels and don't offer the kind of control you need to make a fancy twist.

**Zest tool**—This is a purely bar-application tool. It is designed to make long loops of citrus zest that look beautiful in long drinks like the Collins. It's not a must-have tool, but it will save you time and impress your friends.

**Muddler**—Anything, from a spatula handle or a teaspoon can serve as a muddler, but a dedicated tool will come in handy for making a lot of Mojitos. Stay away from wooden ones. You can't put them in the dishwasher, and they require a lot of hand cleaning because they are porous and hold onto mashed bits of ingredients that become breeding grounds for bacteria. Get a metal muddler if you get anything.

**Citrus juicer**—These simple lever tools really take the struggle out of juicing. Get a metal one with a strong hinge. Juicing limes for margaritas really takes a toll on plastic juicers. If you use the ream-and-bowl type of juicer, you'll find that limes are a challenge, but you will be able to juice halves of oranges and grapefruit with no problem. I recommend getting both to give you the most versatility.

**Lewis bag**—Before I got one of these, I used a clean cotton dish towel to hold ice cubes while I smashed them with a meat tenderizer. I lost a lot of the ice, which sticks to the cotton. A canvas Lewis bag will not hold onto the crushed ice, allowing you to make crushed ice cocktails without needing a blender. I still use a meat tenderizer, but there are inexpensive wooden mallets available that will do the trick.

## Note on Types of Ice

The recipes in this book will refer to several types of ice when shaking or blending cocktails. If the recipe says "fill with ice" or "full of ice," it can be assumed to be ice cubes from a typical ice cube tray. "Crushed ice" is required for drinks like the mint julep where greater ice melt and quick cooling of fine bits of ice are critical for the drinking experience. You can make crushed ice with an ice machine or blender, but I often just use my mallet and Lewis bag if the cocktail I'm making (a mint julep, for example) isn't blended. A good rule of thumb for the amount of crushed ice per drink is one whole standard ice cube tray.

"Cracked ice" is somewhere between the whole cubes and crushed. You can make it using a mallet and the Lewis bag if you're in a hurry. Just whack a handful of cubes in the bag a few times to break it into smaller chunks. These chunks have more total surface area that make them useful for shaking cocktails that require more dilution and a faster chill. When blending, cracked is very important because whole ice cubes take a long time to chip. If you dump whole cubes into your blender with the cocktail and blend, you will get soupy, diluted cocktail with large, ugly hunks of ice. Blending longer only slightly decreases the size of the ice hunks and leaves you with a totally watery and nearly flavorless cocktail. When blending using ice from a tray, crack them first in the Lewis bag to save you the aggravation.

**Ice cube trays and molds**—Believe it or not, the ice made in ice cube trays is superior to an ice machine ice when it comes to cocktails. Even your basic ice cube tray will produce clearer ice that looks more attractive than the stuff that comes out of an icemaker. Refrigerator ice machines make cloudy, aerated ice that tastes stale when it melts. But the biggest drawback of ice machine ice is that they block the lip of your glass when you lift it to drink. No one enjoys this, so having several trays of ice in your freezer and a container you can empty the trays into when they are frozen is the best way to stock ice for your party. If you prefer to make large cubes or spheres of ice for fancy rocks cocktails, there are plenty of options and all work well. Having a few handy will impress your guests, but you will run out of them quickly if you rely on them for a majority of drinks you plan to make.

**Blender**—You don't need a fancy ice blending machine if you only make blended drinks from time to time. Even if you are a big fan of frozen margaritas, a quality blender with an ice crush setting will serve you well. My Cuisinart blender has lasted me through twenty years and an untold number of blended drinks and is still kicking.

## Glassware

**Where to buy:** department store or kitchen supply store
**What to buy:** at least four of each of the following: cocktail (martini glasses), highball or Collins glasses, old-fashioned glasses, pint glasses, champagne flutes, and stemmed wine glasses.

Don't be fooled into thinking that a home bar has to have stacks of every kind of drinking container that a restaurant bar has. There's no way you will need twenty of any type of glass unless you like dusting. The above recommendation is, if anything, somewhat liberal. You can easily make do with four of each type of glass or omit a type entirely if you have no intention of using it. But it is good to keep in mind that the drinking experience can be enhanced with the proper shape of glass, and serving some drinks in the wrong glass can ruin a cocktail.

**Cocktail glass**—This category of glass includes martini glasses and coupes—stemmed glasses with a broad rim exposing a large surface area under the drinker's nose. These are used for martinis, Manhattans, sidecars, and some sours, which means they will be one of your most useful purchases. If you prefer the angular look of the 1980s martini glass, get these or make up your four cocktail glass collection with two martini glasses and two coupes.

**Highball or Collins glass**—These will be your tall drink glasses for daisies, Collins, and general spirit and soda mixers. They can double as a beer glass for pilsners and make good containers for spritzes, fizzes, and punches.

**Old-fashioned glass**—A rocks glass, or the chunkier old-fashioned glass, is more than a drink-specific glass. This one gets used for all spirits-forward cocktails served with ice. Beyond the old-fashioned, it will be perfect for margaritas (on the rocks) and some sours as well as being your standard whiskey glass. For that reason, think of the recommended four glasses being a minimum. If you serve whiskey often, you'll want more of these.

**Pint glass**—Besides being your main beer glass, a pint glass is necessary for beer cocktails like the michelada and will be useful for serving larger portions of Bloody Marys. Blended cocktails and tropical drinks with crushed ice can be served in both pint glasses or highball glasses. The pint also forms half of the Boston shaker tin.

**Champagne flute**—You know best how many people you need to serve a champagne toast to, so buy enough of these to suit your needs. But the champagne flute is also used in champagne cocktails like the St-Germain cocktail. Not having the glass would detract from the cocktail's look and the overall drinking experience, so have a few of these for special occasions.

**Stemmed wine glasses**—Obviously you will need these for wine service, but some cocktails go in wine glasses as well. Consider getting a variety of wine glasses with different size bowls for different purposes. A white wine glass works well as a sour glass; its narrow rim increases the height that the egg white foam will stand above the liquid. A wide-lipped glass with a shorter stem can be a fun way to serve a blended cocktail, a spritz, or a brandy or sherry. Smaller stemmed cordial glasses are wonderful for serving port or amari. A stemless glass makes for a good snifter or rocks glass.

**Sour Glass or Snifter**—This low-stem glass is more of an accessory to certain kinds of drinks and can up your cocktail game. It's rare to find a made-to-purpose whiskey sour glass anymore. These short stemmed glasses were designed to allow egg white foam to rise and required the drinker to sip through the foam, with its lemony scent and acidity until you could get to the sweet cocktail beneath. There will be few times such a glass is necessary and I find it better to have glasses that can serve a dual purpose. The Glencairn glass works very well for a sour glass, but it is made for tasting whiskey and scotch neat. A snifter can serve the same dual purpose and might be easier to find then the Glencairn. Snifters have the added benefit of being a perfect container for a blended cocktail like a margarita or frozen daiquiri.

# I LIKE MY MARYS BLOODY

There is something to be said for the sublime refreshment you get from a savory cocktail. The Bloody Mary is sort of the ringleader of a gang of spicy hangover helpers. That's right, an entire family of cocktails were invented to help drinkers cope with the morning after. When viewed in this light, the Bloody Mary makes a lot of sense: salt and tomato juice replenish electrolytes lost from drinking the night before, and a shot of vodka alleviates the headache associated with withdraw from alcohol. They also pair surprisingly well with breakfast foods like eggs, bacon, and fried potatoes. But a Bloody Mary's charm isn't only for morning drinking. Some die-hard fans of this cocktail enjoy them all day long.

The thing that sets a Bloody Mary apart from many hangover drinks, like the Corpse Reviver series, is that they aren't sweet. What started out as a hasty liquor and tomato juice cocktail in an old-fashioned glass blossomed into what is often regarded as the world's most complicated cocktail. Aside from a dozen ingredients in the tomato-based mix, you can now find outlandishly garnished pint glasses of Bloody Marys—pizza slices, soft pretzels, king crab legs, and even a roasted chicken have appeared atop this once humble cocktail. Clearly, restaurants know how to appeal to a drinker's impaired judgement when they are suffering from a hangover.

The important thing to keep in mind when bartending at home is that your Bloody Mary can be as simple or as complicated as you want. You can handmake them from scratch, or you can buy a mix. Garnishes are unnecessary and even a distraction, but you can go all out with a bacon salt rim and a smorgasbord of snacks to garnish your glass. It's really only a question of commitment: how much time and worry do you want to put into your drink when you feel you really need the relief of a Bloody Mary or one of its family members?

# Bloody Marys

## Bloody Mary Master Recipe

Below is the basic template for this most complicated cocktail. Keep in mind that this recipe uses four ounces of canned tomato juice, not a mix that contains a lot of seasoning of its own. To avoid reprinting the whole list of ingredients for each modification, I'll simply suggest what to add in and what to take out. Unless a garnish is specified, feel free to improvise. Some good suggestions include dill pickles, olives, bacon, celery sticks, cocktail onions, pickled beets, and cilantro. A kosher salt or celery salt rim is also a good move. If you don't have celery salt, simply add equal parts celery seeds to your kosher salt in the dipping saucer.

> 2 oz. vodka
> 4 oz. tomato juice
> ½ tsp. lemon juice
> ½ tsp. Worcestershire sauce
> ½ tsp. horseradish sauce
> 4–8 dashes Tabasco sauce
> pinch of ground pepper
> pinch of kosher salt
> lime wedge to garnish

Combine all ingredients in a shaker with ice. Shake and strain into a highball glass (no ice) and garnish with a lime wedge.

# Bloody Mary Modifications

Of course, you can choose to add or remove ingredients as you see fit. That's the beauty of this cocktail. Using different sauces like barbecue or a juice mix like V8 changes the template, while Clamato can be used in lieu of some of the citrus and spice as it comes bottled with its own. Below you'll see recipes that include beer, beef bouillon, and clam juice, as well as suggestions for changing the main spirit to something richer than vodka for a different kind of experience.

**Acapulco Clam Digger**—Use tequila in place of vodka and add 3 oz. clam juice to the master recipe. Rim an old-fashioned glass with coarse salt like a margarita and garnish with a lime wheel.

**Bloody Bull**—A beefier Bloody Mary. Use the master recipe and add 4 oz. of cold beef bouillon.

**Bloody Caesar**—This is the variation that introduced the celery stick. It is milder than the original: replace Tabasco sauce for a pinch of cayenne pepper and omit the horseradish.

**Bloody Maria**—Use tequila and lime juice in place of vodka and lemon juice in the master recipe. Serve in a highball glass rimmed with coarse salt and garnish with a lime wedge.

**Buddy's Bloody Mary**—Add a tsp. of barbeque sauce in a shaker full of ice along with 2 oz. of vodka and 4 oz. of V8 juice.

**Bull Shot**—Use 4 oz. beef bouillon in place of tomato juice in the master recipe. For the **Cock and Bull Shot** use equal parts chicken and beef bouillon in place of tomato juice in the master recipe.

**Canadian Dog's Nose**—The name is as intriguing as is the recipe. It's a Canadian michelada with Canadian whisky.

> 2 oz. Canadian whisky (Black Velvet Special Reserve recommended)
> 1 tsp. Worcestershire sauce
> 4–8 dashes Tabasco sauce
> 4 oz. tomato juice
> 6 oz. lager beer (like Molson or Labatt Blue)
> salt and black pepper, to garnish

Combine whisky, tomato juice, and sauces in a shaker with ice. Shake and pour into a pint glass. Add beer while stirring slowly. Sprinkle salt and pepper on top.

**Cold and Clammy Bloody Mary**— Use Clamato instead of tomato juice in the master recipe and garnish with green onion stems.

**Connemara Clammer**—Substitute Irish Whiskey for the vodka in the master recipe and add 2 oz. clam juice.

**Ginza Mary**—Add 1½ oz. sake to the master recipe and replace Worcestershire sauce with several dashes of soy sauce.

**Michelada**—It's a Mexican favorite combining beer and Bloody Mary ingredients. The Michelada is a great low-alcohol cocktail (about half a beer) that is salty and refreshing.

> 1 bottle of lager or pilsner-style beer
> 2 oz. tomato juice
> 1 oz. lime juice
> several dashes of hot sauce

Rim the top of a pilsner or pint glass with salt by first coating it in lime juice. Fill the glass with ice and pour a light beer into the glass until it is more than halfway full. Squeeze half a lime into the glass and top it off with tomato juice and several dashes of hot sauce.

## "We're Making Bloody Mary Mix for the Masses!"

There's no reason the home bartender is required to make every Bloody Mary from scratch. Most bars don't, so why should you? Brands of Mary mix you can find in the store are all pretty good, but most don't come with horseradish or very much chili spice, so modify the mix to your taste. The best brands I've found are McClure's Spicy Bloody Mary, Zing Zang, Mr & Mrs T, and Demitri's. I also like Clamato when I need to add clam juice and don't want to buy it separately. These are all helpful time savers that will make your home bar Bloody Mary-ready in case you get the urge to have one.

But mixes have varying shelf lives once they are opened. Cracking a 32 oz. bottle for one drink is a bit of a waste. If this is a reoccurring problem, buy small cans of tomato juice and batch Bloody Mary ingredients in sealable containers. Most of the ingredients in Bloody Mary mix are shelf stable—salt, pepper, Worcestershire sauce, and celery salt can be stored in jars, ready for single servings that only require fresh citrus, Tabasco, and horseradish to be added.

Alternatively, you can batch enough shelf-stable ingredients in a large container to accommodate a 32 oz. can of tomato juice. This is the perfect way to prep for a brunch party. Put 2 tbsp. each of black pepper, kosher salt, and 1 oz. Tabasco sauce in a sealable container with 2 oz. Worcestershire sauce. You don't even have to save your Mary pre-mix in a large container. A small plastic container will hold the dry ingredients and Worcestershire sauce. Just open it when you need it, plop the ingredients into a pitcher of tomato juice, and stir.

**Moonshot**—While not really a Bloody Mary, the moonshot is a savory hangover cure with a spicy and clammy finish that is oddly satisfying. This is a short drink designed to be consumed in one gulp like a shot.

> 2 oz. gin (London dry gin like Beefeater)
> 3 oz. clam juice
> 1 dash Tabasco sauce

Combine all ingredients in a mixing glass with ice. Stir and strain into an old-fashioned glass full of fresh ice.

**Oresund**—This Danish/Swedish Bloody Mary has a few modifications to make it more Nordic. Most noticeably, it substitutes the Scandinavian spirit akvavit (or aquavit) for vodka to give it a strong herbal taste.

> 2 oz. akvavit (aquavit)
> 2 oz. V8 juice
> 2 oz. tomato juice
> 2 oz. clam juice
> ½ tsp. lemon juice
> ½ tsp. Worcestershire sauce
> pinch of finely chopped dill
> pinch of finely chopped parsley
> sprig of fresh dill, to garnish

Combine all ingredients except for garnish in a Collins or highball glass full of ice and stir. Garnish with the dill sprig.

**Prairie Oyster**—This is a strange offshoot from the Bloody Mary family designed to cure a hangover quickly. It has the protein of a raw egg and the liquor and spice necessary to open the eyes of the afflicted. Not for the faint of heart.

> 2 oz. brandy
> ½ oz. red wine vinegar
> ½ oz. Worcestershire sauce
> 1 tsp. ketchup
> 1 dash Tabasco sauce
> 1 dash ground cayenne pepper, to garnish
> 1 egg yolk

Combine all ingredients except egg yolk and cayenne pepper in a shaker with ice. Shake and strain into a chilled old-fashioned glass. Float egg yolk on top and dust with cayenne pepper.

**Smokin' Texas Mary**—Add 1 oz. smoky barbecue sauce to the juices and a pickled jalapeno as garnish.

**Steaming Bull**—The hot version of a Bloody Bull. Add 4 oz. beef bouillon to the master recipe mix (alcohol omitted) and warm in a saucepan over medium heat until steaming. Pour 2 oz. of vodka or tequila in a hot beverage mug and top with hot mix from the saucepan.

## My Bloody Mary Recipe

_____

_____

_____

_____

_____

_____

_____

_____

_____

_____

# A CHAIN OF DAISIES

What cocktail do you make for a friend who says they don't like hard liquor? As a bartender, that was a puzzle I had to face about once a day. When mixing at home, I encountered friends and neighbors who either seldom drank, had no idea what their liquor preferences were, or admitted that they may have never had a real cocktail before. You can't ask someone like this what they would like; you have to take the bull by the horns. If you encounter a drinker as green as the one I've described, you need to come up with a drink on the spot that will please anyone. I encourage you to introduce them to Miss Daisy.

At first glance, the daisy is an unusual drink to deserve notice, much less an entire section of a cocktail book: It's not as well-known as the margarita; it doesn't specify a popular spirit like bourbon in the way an old-fashioned does, and it's not as simple a recipe as a highball or gin and tonic. But I believe that the daisy is the perfect go-to drink for new bartenders and beginning cocktail drinkers alike.

The daisy is a strong, tart, and fizzy delight to drink. Grenadine, the sweetener in most recipes, is colorful, and the soda bubbles look dynamic in a highball glass. The basic recipe is a good size glug of a hard liquor, a sugar syrup like grenadine, lemon juice for tartness, and a top-off of sparkling water. Any number of garnishes can be used to make it look and smell even more appealing. Did I mention it's strong? Three ounces of the principal liquor make it equal to what sophisticated martini drinkers are fond of ordering, but it tastes much lighter when combined with juice and soda. In short, the daisy is designed to please as many people as possible. And though it is great to drink on a hot day, the interchangeability of the daisy's ingredients make it a good recipe to know in all seasons.

The best part about the daisy for the experienced bartender is the way it can be used to impress your guests. The picky drinker might be satisfied with a hard seltzer, but handing them a can of White Claw undermines your bartending ability. Make them a daisy with a spirit they are curious to try and get them to stretch their cocktail comfort zone. They'll love it and, when you make them a second daisy with a different spirit, you'll have proven your skill.

# Daisies

## Daisy Master Recipe

Gin is the base of the original daisy because it was the main mixing spirit in the pre-Prohibition days. You'll want to use a London dry gin like Tanqueray to understand how the master recipe works. When you get used to that, you can try other gins from Europe and the US to find your favorite.

Grenadine is critical to most daisy recipes, and, for consistency, I urge you to buy a bottle rather than attempt to make it from fresh pomegranate seeds or POM juice, which tend to make a syrup that has a cooked fruit taste and a brown color. It's better if your sweetener is bright and fresh tasting. Of course, Rose's grenadine is the most widely available and is fine to use, but you can go craftier with Liber & Co. Real Grenadine or Powell & Mahoney's True Grenadine. These are available at wine shops and organic grocers and are worth seeking out.

> 3 oz. gin (London dry, like Beefeater)
> 1 oz. lemon juice
> ½ oz. grenadine
> 1 tsp. simple syrup
> Sparkling water
> orange slice, to garnish

Combine all liquid ingredients except for sparkling water in a shaker with ice and shake to chill. Strain into a highball glass full of fresh ice and top with sparkling water. Stir gently and garnish with the orange slice.

# Modifications

The daisy is an extremely modifiable formula, limited only by the spirits available to the bartender. The standard gin daisy could just as easily be made as a vodka daisy or a rum daisy with light rum. But why stop there? Try a white tequila daisy, or get really creative and sub in white fruit brandies like pisco, grappa, or kirschwasser. If you chose an aged spirit like whiskey, dark rum, or brandy, know that the flavor will be richer due to the aging of the spirit in oak barrels. Apple brandy or applejack makes a particularly autumnal tasting daisy that can be improved by using apple slices for garnishes. Some recipes go farther than simply swapping out the main spirit. I've included my favorites, as well as a few kissing cousins of the original.

**Berta's Special**—This daisy cousin is a rare tequila substitution.

> 2 oz. gold tequila (I recommend Sauza Añejo)
> 1 oz. lime juice
> 1 egg white
> 5–7 dashes of orange bitters
> sparkling water
> lime slice, to garnish

Combine the first four ingredients in a shaker with no ice. Shake to produce foam. Add ice and shake to chill and pour into a chilled Collins glass. Top with sparkling water and garnish with the lime slice.

**Bourbon Daisy**—More than just a simple substitution of bourbon, this daisy attempts to capture the quintessence of Southern drinking with a whiff of Southern Comfort. The optional pineapple spear can be made by slicing the fruit lengthwise into sticks. Save the fronds for additional garnishes.

> 1½ oz. bourbon (I recommend Evan Williams
>     Bottled-in-Bond edition)
> ½ oz. lemon juice
> 1 tsp. grenadine
> club soda
> 1 tsp. Southern Comfort
> orange slice and pineapple spear, to garnish (optional)

Combine liquid ingredients except for sparkling water in a shaker with ice. Shake to chill and strain into a highball glass full of fresh ice. Top with soda and stir gently. Garnish with fruit.

**Canadian Daisy**—This recipe specifies Canadian whisky and fresh raspberries as a garnish as well as cooked into the syrup. Making the syrup is not complicated and only requires the addition of raspberries while making a standard simple syrup (see Appendix on syrups and infusions).

> 2 oz. Canadian whisky
> ½ oz. brandy
> ½ oz. lemon juice
> 1 tsp. raspberry syrup
> sparkling water
> fresh raspberries, to garnish

Combine liquid ingredients except for sparkling water in a shaker with ice. Shake to chill and strain into a highball glass full of fresh ice. Top with soda and stir gently. Garnish with several raspberries on a cocktail pick.

**Gin Rickey**—The gin rickey is a sugar-free version of the daisy. Omit all sweetener and use lime juice instead of lemon. No shaking required.

>  2 oz. London dry gin
>  1 oz. lime juice
>  sparkling water

Pour gin and lime juice in a highball glass full of ice. Top with sparkling water and stir gently.

**Manhattan Cooler** (printed in *The New American Bartender's Guide*, 1997)—Coolers are similar to daisies except that they rarely require grenadine as the sweetener. Instead, expect them to use sweet liqueurs like maraschino and amaretto.

>  1½ oz. blended American whiskey
>  ½ oz. French (dry) vermouth
>  ½ oz. amaretto
>  2 oz. lemon juice
>  1 oz. orange juice
>  sparkling water

Combine liquid ingredients except for sparkling water in a shaker with ice. Shake to chill and strain into a highball glass full of fresh ice. Top with sparkling water.

**Mojito**—It's the odd rum cocktail that stands out in this collection of fizzy drinks with its bouquet of fragrant mint leaves. Though it is no different than a minty daisy without grenadine, a great mojito is hard to master. Get the ratio of sugar to lime juice off by a tiny fraction, or use too little ice and too much sparkling water, and you have a mess with wet mint leaves. Make the recipe several times, adjusting to your tastes. Omit the sparkling water altogether or splash Gosling's Black Seal rum on top. Try dusting the mint garnish with powdered sugar or a dash of Angostura bitters and see what that does for the scent of the drink. Just remember that there is no one right way to make a mojito, but there are a lot of ways it can go wrong. If that happens, don't get discouraged. Try it again and again until you and your guests are satisfied.

> 10 mint leaves
> 2 oz. light rum (I use Cruzan white rum)
> 1 oz. simple syrup
> 1 oz. lime juice
> sparkling water (No more than the top quarter
>     of the glass once ice is added to the top)
> mint sprig, to garnish

Gently muddle mint leaves and simple syrup in a shaker. Add lime juice, rum, and ice, and shake to chill. Strain into a chilled highball or double old-fashioned glass full of cracked ice. Top the glass with more cracked ice and add a splash or more of sparkling water. Garnish with a mint sprig.

**Moscow Mule**—This cocktail was made famous in the 1950s and, consequently, introduced vodka to the American bar scene. Critical to its appeal was the copper mule cup. This cup transferred heat out of the liquid very quickly and produced a pleasing frosted mug effect when filled with crushed ice.

> 2 oz. vodka
> ½ oz. lime juice
> ginger beer
> lime wedge and mint sprig, to garnish (optional)

Add vodka and lime juice to a shaker with ice. Shake and then strain into a mule glass packed with crushed ice. Add ginger beer until the mug is three quarters full, and top with more ice to create a low mound of ice. Garnish with lime wedge and mint sprig and serve with a straw.

**Paloma**—This daisy variation will please any tequila drinker. It's the second most popular tequila cocktail, but it is closer to a daisy than a margarita.

> 2 oz. white tequila (I recommend Sauza Blanco)
> ½ oz. lime juice
> Italian grapefruit soda
> 1 tsp. simple syrup
> coarse salt, to rim
> sparkling water

Rim a highball glass by rubbing it with a slice of lime and dipping it in a saucer of salt. Add tequila, simple syrup, lime juice, and ice to the glass. Top with grapefruit soda and stir gently.

**The White Witch**—This refreshing rum drink is a cross between a mojito and a dessert cocktail. Curaçao and crème de cacao give it the flavor of a chocolate orange, and mint dusted with powdered sugar makes for a beautiful presentation.

> 1 oz. light rum
> ½ oz. (white) curaçao
> ½ oz. crème de cacao
> juice of ½ lime
> sparkling water or club soda
> mint sprig coated in powdered sugar, to garnish

Shake liquors on ice in a shaker and strain into a Collins or highball glass full of fresh ice. Squeeze the juice of a lime half on top and stir. Top the drink with sparkling water or club soda and garnish with a sprig of mint coated in powdered sugar.

*My Daisy Recipe*

_____

_____

_____

_____

_____

_____

_____

_____

# Fizzes

 A fizz, either with egg white or without, is vigorously shaken to create a fizzy foam on top of the glass. Special attention must be paid to the shaking process to achieve this effect.

**Ramos Fizz**—The deluxe gin fizz of New Orleans fame. This recipe is a perfect example of when it is necessary to do a dry shake with all ingredients except ice and then add ice and shake an additional thirty times to chill and aerate the ingredients to maintain the foam. According to New Orleans tradition, one should shake for nine minutes, but that is more of a gimmick than a fact. A prolonged second shake with ice will give you the fluffy foam that is so firm it should hold your straw without it touching the sides of the glass.

> 3 oz. gin
> 1 egg white
> ½ oz. lemon juice
> ½ oz. lime juice
> ½ oz. half-and-half
> 3–5 dashes orange blossom water (This inexpensive
>     ingredient can be found in the baking aisle in
>     most supermarkets.)
> sparkling water

Combine all ingredients except half-and-half and sparkling water in a shaker. Shake vigorously to create foam. Add ice and half-and-half and shake again until chilled. Strain the ice out of the shaker while preserving the liquid ingredients for a third shake. Pour into a chilled Collins glass and top with sparkling water. A successful Ramos fizz can be topped with sparkling water until a fluffy foam head rises a half inch or more above the glass, and a straw inserted into its center will not move.

**Chicago Fizz**—Egg white adds a silky texture to this bubbly beverage.

> 1½ oz. gold rum (try Bacardi Gold)
> 1 oz. port wine
> ½ oz. lemon juice
> ½ tsp. sugar
> 1 egg white
> sparkling water

Combine all ingredients except sparkling water in a shaker with ice. Shake vigorously and strain into chilled Collins or highball glass full of fresh ice. Top with sparkling water and stir gently.

**Georgia Peach Fizz**—Consider doing this cocktail when peaches are in season!

> 2 oz. brandy (I like Korbel)
> 1 oz. peach brandy (peach schnapps is an acceptable substitute)
> ½ oz. crème de bananes
> 1 oz. lemon juice
> 1 tsp. simple syrup
> sparkling water
> peach slice, to garnish

Combine liquors, lemon juice, and simple syrup in a mixing glass with ice. Stir and pour into a chilled Collins or highball glass. Top with sparkling water and stir gently. Garnish with the peach slice.

**Peach Blow Fizz**—This peach fizz relies on fresh fruit instead of liqueurs to provide fruity flavors.

> 3 oz. gin
> 1 oz. lemon juice
> 1 oz. half-and-half
> 1 tsp. simple syrup (homemade peach syrup is ideal)
> 5 ripe strawberries (hulled and sliced)
> ¼ peach, diced
> sparkling water
> peach slice, to garnish

Muddle strawberries, diced peach, and simple syrup in a shaker until well mashed. Add gin and lemon juice and shake with ice until chilled. Add half-and-half and shake vigorously. Pour into a chilled highball glass. Top with soda, stir, and garnish with a peach slice.

## My Fizz Recipe

---
---
---
---
---
---
---
---
---

# Spritz

A spritz is a fizzy, wine-based cocktail that gets its bubbles from the addition of either sparkling water, sparkling wine or both. Below are some of the most popular spritz cocktails. Glassware for spritzes can be flexible. You can stick with the typical highball glass or change things up with a wine glass or champagne flute. I've suggested my favorites in the following recipes.

**Aperol Spritz**—This is the perfect opportunity to use the Aperol aperitivo mentioned in the section on stocking your bar. You can't do this Italian favorite without it.

> 2 oz. Aperol
> 3 oz. sparkling wine
> 1 oz. sparkling water
> orange slice, to garnish

Pour Aperol into a highball glass full of ice. Add sparkling wine and top with sparkling water. Stir gently and garnish with the orange slice. Serve with a straw.

**French 75**—The original French 75 was made by mixing cognac and champagne with lemon juice and sugar in a champagne flute. Now that gin is the preferred spirit, this cocktail is basically a Collins made with champagne.

> 2 oz. dry gin (or cognac, if you are a traditionalist)
> ½ oz. lemon juice
> ½ oz. simple syrup
> Champagne or sparkling wine
> long lemon twist, to garnish

Combine all ingredients except champagne in a shaker with ice. Shake and strain into a chilled champagne flute or cocktail glass. Top with champagne and garnish with a long twist of zested lemon peel.

**St-Germain Cocktail**—I had to include this lovely champagne cocktail that was designed specifically to showcase the light and floral flavor of France's St-Germain elderflower liqueur. To make this recipe, simply substitute the simple syrup of the French 75 recipe above with St-Germain.

## My Spritz Recipe

_____

_____

_____

_____

_____

_____

_____

## "Who Is that Tom Collins Guy?"

It all began in the 1860s with the John Collins, a cocktail invented by a London coffee house headwaiter of the same name. The original recipe used Old Tom or Holland genever gin as the main spirit. By the time the drink made its way to America, the cocktail had become known as the Tom Collins. The new gin cocktail was very popular with American drinkers, some of whom used the name to propagate a hoax against bar guests.

The hoax, intended to make the victim appear ridiculous, initiated when the hoaxers would ask the target if they had seen Tom Collins. When the dupe replied they did not know a Tom Collins, the hoaxer would say that Collins was speaking slander about the person. Other bar patrons who were in on the ruse would submit that Tom Collins could be found at a different establishment nearby, causing the target to anxiously seek out a fictitious person. This practical joke became so common that in 1874, several New York and Pennsylvania newspapers printed articles reporting Tom Collins sightings. Ironically, the Tom Collins cocktail could be spotted simultaneously at many bars at the time.

---

**Tom Collins**—Probably the best-known member of the daisy family is the Tom Collins. These cocktails are basically daisies without grenadine that are served in their signature glassware. If you have a Collins glass, use it when you make a Tom Collins. Like the old-fashioned glass or mule cup, they enhance the drinking experience.

> 3 oz. London dry gin
> 2 oz. lemon juice
> ½ oz. simple syrup
> sparkling water
> orange slice and maraschino cherry, to garnish

Combine all ingredients except sparkling water in a shaker with ice. Shake to chill and strain into a highball or Collins glass and top with sparkling water. Stir gently and garnish with fruit.

**Rum Collins**—Substitute light (lightly aged) rum for gin in the Tom Collins recipe.

**Tequila Collins**—Substitute white tequila for gin in the Tom Collins recipe.

**Vodka Collins**—Substitute vodka for gin in the Tom Collins recipe.

**Whiskey Collins**—Substitute blended whiskey for gin in the Tom Collins recipe.

## My Collins Recipe

_____

_____

_____

_____

_____

_____

_____

_____

_____

# DAIQUIRIS, MARGARITAS, & THE DEBATE OVER BLENDING

On the surface, a daiquiri and a margarita have a lot in common: they are both tart lime-juice drinks, they utilize flavorful spirits that come from countries surrounded by the Caribbean Sea, and you can often find them both in rocks and blended ice formats. Why some cocktail nerds decided that that these two similar drinks belong to different families is beyond me. I suspect it has a little to do with cocktail purists' disdain for tequila—the margarita being a recent invention, while the daiquiri has been around since the colonial rum trade.

I'm not interested in classifying cocktails into families. My goal is to help home bartenders find cocktail recipes that are similar to what they already like. From that perspective, it's better to anticipate what drinks will be called for on a particular occasion. I imagine pool parties and barbecues where Latin pop musing is playing and daiquiris are being served would also be prime environments for margarita mixing as well. To have one and not the other would almost seem obtuse.

The cocktails in this section are tart and fruity. They make use of funky and earthy spirits made from cane sugar and agave plants grown in warm climates. And whether you choose to serve them neat, on the rocks, or blended, they contribute tremendously to the party atmosphere.

# Daiquiris

## Daiquiri Master Recipe

The original daiquiri is a sour lime juice and rum cocktail that is served up, meaning in a cocktail glass with no ice. This format lends itself well to richer tasting rums that carry some of the sweet scent of the sugar or funk of the cane from which it was distilled. For that reason, I recommend Plantation 3 Stars blended white rum or Flor de Caña 4 Extra Seco white rum. A Martinique Rhum Agricole may also be used if you prefer a daiquiri with fresh sugarcane notes.

> 2 oz. lightly aged white rum (like Plantation 3 Stars)
> ¾ oz. lime juice
> ¾ oz. simple syrup
> lime wedge, to garnish

Shake all liquid ingredients with plenty of ice. Double strain into a chilled cocktail glass and garnish with a lime wedge.

## Modifications

Aside from the obvious changes in presentation—serving on the rocks or frozen—daiquiri variations usually involve introducing fresh fruit or fruit juice to change the flavor. Change the main spirit to gin or vodka, however, and it becomes the classic gimlet! More often than not, a "flavored" daiquiri will have additional liqueurs in it, especially when served frozen. Juice flavors tend to get lost in frozen drinks unless they are concentrated in a sugar syrup or a liqueur. Expect to experiment with how much fruit, simple syrup, and additional spirits suit your taste when blending daiquiris.

**Apple Daiquiri**—This cocktail can be served up, on the rocks in a highball glass, or frozen.

> 2 oz. light rum
> ¾ oz. apple brandy
> ½ oz. lemon juice
> 2 tsp. simple syrup
> apple slice, to garnish

Combine all ingredients except apple slice in a shaker or blender with ice. Shake or blend and pour into a chilled highball glass.

**Banana Daiquiri**—Make this cocktail with slightly green bananas to create a different tropical experience.

> 2 oz. light rum
> ½ oz. lime juice
> ½ oz. triple sec
> ½ oz. half-and-half
> 1 tsp. sugar
> ¼ banana, sliced
> lime slice, to garnish

Combine all ingredients except lime slice in a blender with cracked ice. Blend until smooth and pour into a balloon wine glass. Garnish with lime slice.

**Cherry Daiquiri**—Change the original recipe up by adding cherry spirits like kirschwasser and Cherry Heering.

> 2 oz. light rum
> ½ oz. cherry liqueur (I use Cherry Heering)
> ½ oz. lime juice
> ¼ tsp. kirschwasser
> lime twist, to garnish

Combine all ingredients except lime twist in a shaker with ice. Shake and strain into a chilled cocktail glass. Garnish with the lime twist.

**Derby Daiquiri**—More about presentation than ingredients, this drink is named after a popular hat.

> 2 oz. light rum (use Cruzan aged rum)
> ½ oz. lime juice
> 1 oz. orange juice
> 1 tsp. sugar

Combine all ingredients in a blender with cracked ice. Blend until slushy and pour into a chilled champagne flute.

**Frozen Daiquiri**—This is the blended version of the master recipe. It is very tart, but feel free to adjust the sugar content to your taste.

> 2 oz. light rum
> ¾ oz. lime juice
> ½ tsp. sugar
> lime slice, to garnish

Combine all ingredients except lime slice in a blender with ½ cup cracked ice. Blend slowly until smooth but not watery. Pour into a champagne flute, balloon wine glass, or cocktail glass and garnish with lime slice.

**Frozen Guava Daiquiri**—Guava nectar can be purchased in most grocery stores.

> 1½ oz. light rum (try it with Plantation 3 Stars)
> ½ oz. lime juice
> 1 oz. guava nectar
> 1 tsp. crème de bananes (or Cruzan banana rum)
> lime slice, to garnish

Combine all ingredients except lime slice in a blender with ice. Blend until smooth and pour into a deep champagne or stemless wine glass. Garnish with lime slice.

**Frozen Mint Daiquiri**—Blending mint leaves works if the mixture is well-blended and the leaves are only visible as tiny pieces. A splash of green crème de menthe will improve the appearance of this drink if you serve it in a clear glass. Otherwise, an opaque tiki mug is a good choice.

> 2 oz. light rum
> 1 oz. lime juice
> 6 mint leaves
> 1 tsp. sugar
> 1 splash green crème de menthe (optional)
> mint sprig and lime slice, to garnish

Combine all ingredients except garnishes in a blender with cracked ice. Blend until smooth and pour into a Collins glass or tiki mug. If you have more mint and lime slices on hand, garnish at will.

**Frozen Peach Daiquiri**—I recommend making this daiquiri only in peach season or the fruit flavor won't translate as well.

> 2 oz. light rum
> 1 oz. lime juice
> ½ oz. simple syrup
> ½ peach, peeled and diced
> peach wedge, to garnish

Combine all ingredients except garnish in a blender with cracked ice. Blend until smooth and pour into a chilled wine goblet. Garnish with peach wedge.

**Frozen Pineapple Daiquiri**—This frozen daiquiri is a great opportunity to hollow out a pineapple shell to use for your container. Cut the top of the pineapple off, and use a long knife to core it. Use chunks from the inside of the fruit to make the cocktail and syrup (see page 153). Save a sliver of pineapple to make a garnish, or simply put the top back on and drink with a straw.

> 2 oz. light rum
> 1 oz. lime juice
> 2 oz. fresh pineapple chunks
> ½ tsp. pineapple syrup
> pineapple spear, to garnish

Combine all ingredients except for pineapple spear in a blender with cracked ice and blend until smooth. Pour into a cocktail glass and garnish with pineapple spear. (Alternatively, serve in the cored pineapple shell.)

**Frozen Strawberry Daiquiri**—This cocktail was so ubiquitous in the 1980s that one almost forgot that a daiquiri could be made without strawberries. It led to the trend of bars having blenders to meet the strawberry daiquiri demand. See what all the excitement was about.

> 2 oz. light rum
> 1 oz. lime juice
> 1 tsp. sugar
> 7 large strawberries, cored and chopped
> 1 strawberry, to garnish

Blend all ingredients with cracked ice (about 2 cups) except one strawberry saved for garnishing. Pour in a chilled cocktail glass or wine goblet. Garnish with the remaining strawberry.

**Greta Garbo**—This classic cocktail is named after the Swedish-American actress. It uses Pernod to provide a hint of anise flavor and Luxardo Maraschino liqueur for its bright cherry and almond notes. If you have a star anise, float it on top as a garnish to make a drink that looks fit for a star of Garbo's caliber.

> 1½ oz. light rum
> ¼ oz. Luxardo Maraschino liqueur
> ½ oz. simple syrup
> 1 oz. lime juice
> 1 tsp. Pernod
> anise star, to garnish (optional)

Combine liquid ingredients in a shaker with ice. Shake and strain into a chilled cocktail glass. Garnish with the anise star.

**Hemingway Daiquiri**—Named after the famous twentieth-century author, this classic should be enjoyed up with a lime or grapefruit peel twist.

> 1½ oz. white rum (I prefer El Dorado)
> ¼ oz. Luxardo Maraschino liqueur
> ½ oz. grapefruit juice
> ½ oz. lime juice
> ¼ oz. simple syrup
> lime or grapefruit peel, to garnish

Combine all ingredients except fruit peel in a shaker with crushed ice. Shake and strain into a chilled cocktail glass. Garnish with a lime or grapefruit peel.

**Strega Daiquiri**—Strega is an Italian alpine spirit flavored with herbs and fruits. It has a brilliant saffron color and a minty herbal flavor.

> 1 oz. Strega
> 1 oz. light rum (I like Flor de Cana 4 Extra Seco)
> ½ oz. orange juice
> ½ oz. lemon juice
> ½ tsp. orgeat, to taste
> maraschino cherry, to garnish

Combine liquid ingredients in a shaker with ice. Shake and strain into a chilled cocktail glass. Garnish with a cherry.

## My Daiquiri Recipe

_____

_____

_____

_____

_____

_____

_____

_____

# Margaritas

## Margarita Master Recipe

 The original margarita recipe is also served up, but in a glass with a salt rim. The proportion of lime juice in a margarita is greater than it is in a daiquiri. The addition of triple sec is what differentiates a margarita from the family of sours to which the daiquiri belongs. Triple sec or curaçao, a similar Caribbean orange spirit, provides a tantalizing bittersweet orange flavor that plays especially well with aged tequilas. Use simple syrup or agave syrup to taste when you serve this drink up. Increase the amount of syrup to ¾ oz. if you blend it.

> 3 oz. silver tequila (Patrón Silver is an obvious choice)
> 1 oz. triple sec
> 2 oz. lime juice
> ½ oz. simple syrup
> coarse salt, to rim
> lime wedge, to garnish

Make a salt rim by rubbing a lime wedge around the rim of a chilled cocktail glass. Dip the glass into a saucer of coarse salt. Shake all liquid ingredients in a shaker tin with ice. Double strain into the cocktail glass and garnish with the lime wedge.

## Modifications

Just like the daiquiri, margarita variations usually involve fresh fruit and intensely flavored liqueurs. These can be made into frozen or rocks drinks very easily. Play around with different glassware for frozen versions. Sometimes a large wine goblet or a hurricane glass works better when more ice is introduced into the glass.

## "To Blend or Not to Blend?"

I have to admit that I've never worked at a bar that had a blender. That didn't stop me from making some of the best daiquiris and margaritas by using quality spirits and fresh ingredients. Mostly, the objection to blenders in fine dining establishments is the disruptive noise they make. It's one thing to rip a batch of frozen margaritas at a beach bar where there is plenty of background noise, but it is something else entirely when that blender starts up in a white tablecloth restaurant.

The good news is that having a home bar puts the blender decision in your hands. I will give a few bits of advice for buying and operating a blender that I think will serve both novice and veteran bartenders alike.

Start by getting a quality blender that can handle ice. Of course, you could spend a lot of money on a frozen drink mixer found at tiki bars. But if you aren't going for a tiki theme, I recommend a Cuisinart with an "ice crush" function. This is useful for crushing ice ahead of making a swizzle or frozen drinks inside the blender pitcher.

Second, use chipped or cracked ice for blending. Tray ice cubes tend to hang together much longer than you want them to. This creates oddly sized ice balls while the rest of your cocktail is over-diluted. Chipped ice from an ice maker breaks up quickly, shortening your blending time and reducing the chance you will have a watery drink.

Thirdly, use more ice than you think you will need in the glass for each drink. A good rule of thumb is to fill your drink container enough ice to fill the serving container to the top. Doing this will help you measure the amount of ice you need and account for settling that happens when the ice is crushed. It also chills the glass you are about to use and prevents unintended melting that waters down frozen drinks.

Finally, if you take a recipe intended to be served on the rocks and blend it with ice, the sweet and sour balance tends to suffer. To prevent your frozen concoction from being too tart, up the quantity of simple syrup or other sweeteners by one half. Conversely, if you want to take a blender drink recipe and put it on the rocks, you can use half as much sugar. This is a smart move for that skinny margarita-drinking friend. Serve a sugarless margarita neat, and rely on the sweetness of the triple sec to balance the acidity of lime juice.

**Blue Margarita**—Swap blue curaçao for the triple sec in the master recipe.

**Cadillac Margarita**—Restaurants try to upsell guests with this premium margarita recipe. But at your home bar, all your margaritas can be Cadillac-tier. Use an aged tequila like 1800 or Patron Reposado, and swap your ordinary triple sec for a richer cognac-based orange liqueur like Grand Marnier or Royal Combier. Sweeten with agave syrup only.

> 2 oz. 1800 or Patron Reposado tequila
> 2 oz. lime juice
> coarse salt, to rim
> ½ oz. agave syrup
> 1 oz. Grand Marnier
> lime slice, to garnish

Combine all ingredients except Grand Marnier in a shaker with ice. Shake and strain into a salt-rimmed old-fashioned glass. Float Grand Marnier on top and garnish with the lime slice.

**Chapala**—A little thing like the pink color of grenadine and orange juice can really change the experience of this margarita.

> 2 oz. gold tequila (I recommend Sauza Gold)
> ½ oz. triple sec
> 2 oz. orange juice
> 1 oz. lime juice
> ½ oz. grenadine

Combine all ingredients in a shaker with ice. Shake to chill and pour into a highball glass.

**Mexicana**—More tropical than your typical margarita with pineapple juice, which is sweet enough to not require any triple sec.

> 2 oz. silver tequila
> 1 oz. lime juice
> 2 oz. pineapple juice
> ¼ tsp. grenadine

Combine all ingredients in a shaker with ice. Shake and pour into a highball or large old-fashioned glass.

**Peach Margarita**—If you have fresh peaches, use them in a margarita. Add peach chunks to the blender if you do it frozen, but if you are serving it neat, use a store bought peach syrup or jelly instead.

> 2 oz. silver tequila (I recommend Sauza Blanco)
> ½ cup peach slices (optional for blended cocktails)
> ½ oz. peach liqueur or peach schnapps
> ½ oz. triple sec
> 2 oz. lime juice
> 1 tsp. peach syrup or jelly (optional for serving up)
> coarse salt, to rim
> peach slice, to garnish

Combine ingredients including fresh peach chunks with cracked ice in a blender. Blend until smooth and pour into a chilled cocktail glass rimmed with salt. Garnish with a peach slice. (Served neat: Combine all ingredients including peach syrup or jelly in a shaker with ice. Shake and strain into a chilled cocktail glass rimmed with salt. Garnish with a peach slice.)

**Piña**—Sweeter and more tropical than the margarita. No salt rim needed on this drink.

> 2 oz. gold tequila (I recommend Jose Cuervo Gold)
> 3 oz. pineapple juice
> 1 oz. lime juice
> 1 tsp. honey syrup
> lime slice, to garnish

Combine all ingredients except lime slice in a shaker with ice. Shake and strain into a chilled Collins glass. Garnish with lime slice.

**Piñata**—This tart cocktail has a fun candied banana flavor. Give it a swing!

> 2 oz. gold tequila (I recommend Sauza Anejo)
> 1½ oz. lime juice
> 1 oz. crème de bananes (or Cruzan banana rum)
> 1 tsp. simple syrup

Combine all ingredients in a shaker with ice. Shake and strain into a chilled cocktail glass.

**Sauzaliki**—Make this blended margarita variation with fresh banana slices. It's like a tequila smoothie.

> 2 oz. gold tequila (I recommend Sauza Gold)
> 4 oz. orange juice
> 1 tsp. lime juice
> ½ banana, sliced
> ½ oz. simple syrup

Add all ingredients in a blender with cracked ice and blend until smooth. Pour into a cocktail glass or wine goblet.

**Sloe Tequila**—Sloe gin is a sweet fruit gin flavored with the taste of sloe berries (a relative of the plum.) It goes especially well with cucumber.

> 2 oz. white tequila (I recommend Hornitos Silver)
> 1 oz. sloe gin
> ½ oz. lime juice
> 3 cucumber slices, to garnish

Combine tequila, sloe gin, and lime juice in a blender with cracked ice. Blend on low until slushy and pour into an old-fashioned glass. Garnish with cucumber slices on a cocktail pick.

**Strawberry Margarita**—So popular you might mistake it for the classic margarita. I recommend using strawberry syrup made from fresh strawberries (see Appendix on syrups and infusions). That way if you serve it up, you won't have strawberry seeds floating on the surface of the glass.

> 2 oz. silver tequila (I like Tres Agaves)
> 2 oz. lime juice
> ½ oz. strawberry syrup
> ½ oz. triple sec
> coarse salt, to rim
> lime wedge and whole strawberry, to garnish (optional)

Use a lime wedge to rim the cocktail glass with lime juice. Dip it in a plate of coarse salt to coat the rim of the glass with salt. Combine all liquid ingredients in a shaker with ice. Shake and strain into the cocktail glass and garnish with the strawberry and lime wedge.

**Tequila Sunrise**—Sweeter than a margarita but still very popular with tequila drinkers.

> 2 oz. silver tequila
> 3 oz. orange juice
> 1 oz. grenadine

Build drink in a Collins glass with ice and tequila and top with orange juice. Add grenadine to the top, and allow it to sink through the ice for a sunrise visual effect.

## My Margarita Recipe

_____

_____

_____

_____

_____

_____

_____

_____

_____

# DON'T FLIP OUT!
# THE IRREPLACEABLE
# DESSERT DRINK

You might be wondering why an obscure and somewhat dated cocktail like the flip gets prime treatment in this book. It's true you don't see contemporary bars selling whole egg cocktails topped with nutmeg, though the flip is making a comeback on dessert menus.

The flip is important for home bartenders for several reasons. First, it is the quintessential dessert drink. Even without sweet liqueurs that are popular in White Russians and Grasshoppers, a skilled bartender can throw together a spirit and a few ingredients from the kitchen refrigerator that will satisfy a guest's sweet tooth. Furthermore, the flip teaches useful shaking skills for dairy-based cocktails that largely do not involve citrus. Finally, having the flip recipe in your back pocket is good knowledge to apply to many different spirits, whether they be gin, rum, sherry, or a multitude of sweet liqueurs on the market. In short, you are a much more versatile bartender when you can riff on the flip.

The flip enters cocktail history during the colonial rum trade between Europe and the Americas. Hard liquors—at the time these were mostly rums and brandies—were considered a luxury: liquid money. Sugar and grape farmers distilled their perfectly good produce in order to preserve some of the crop in a liquid form that could be sold or bartered. A bumper crop of wine or sugarcane could therefore be converted to a commodity that wouldn't spoil, could be easily transported, and provide extra income.

Rums and brandies were also considered by many to be too intoxicating for unmixed consumption, though certainly they were enjoyed that way. But they didn't pair with dining in the way that wine and beer did, so those who had spirits in stock sought ways to make them more palatable—think rum cakes and brandied pears. But the flip also owes its fame to another colonial luxury: spices.

The British Empire was particularly fond of nutmeg, cinnamon, coffee, and allspice, all of which could be found in equatorial regions across the globe. It was a matter of course that expensive spirits and spices would become part of holiday traditions where lords splurged on guests to conspicuously show off their wealth. But the American colonies were not yet the land of riches that we have come to know today. No one was growing limes or oranges in the cool East Coast climate. It follows that cocktails involving spirits and spice also required what the mostly modest farms produced—you guessed it—dairy and eggs. So, the flip, eggnog, and the lighter milk punch became fashionable cocktails for lavish gatherings.

# Flips

## Flip Master Recipe

The key to the flip is remembering that it is a potent and potable sized eggnog, perfect for a nightcap or dessert. The basic recipe doesn't need to change at all; simply change the spirit and you have a very different experience. Flip glassware is usually a cocktail glass like a champagne coupe or a whiskey sour glass, but feel free to use a slender wine glass.

> 2 oz. brandy or cognac
> 1 whole egg
> ½ oz. half-and-half
> 1 tsp. sugar
> grated nutmeg, to garnish

Combine all ingredients in a shaker without ice. Shake to aerate, then add ice and shake to chill. Strain into a chilled sour or cocktail glass. Garnish with sprinkles of nutmeg.

## Modifications

Try experimenting with the base spirit. Any aged wine or liquor will work. Brandy is probably the most often used spirit, but bourbon, rye, sherry, dark rum, and even gin are all common substitutions. Some sweet liqueurs have made their way into the flip category, and for these, I'll include an entire recipe because the sugar content can change depending on the liqueur. Eggnogs and other spin-offs from the original recipe are fun to try, and ice cream eventually replaces eggs in more modern dessert drinks that take their cues from the flip.

**Coffee Flip**—Coffee is only one ingredient in this blended flip that makes it memorable. Ruby port is an excellent sweetener as well.

> 2 oz. cognac
> 1 oz. ruby port
> 5 oz. cold coffee
> ½ tsp. sugar
> 1 whole egg
> grated nutmeg, to garnish

Combine all ingredients except nutmeg in a blender with ice. Blend until slushy and pour into a chilled wine glass. Sprinkle nutmeg on top.

**Pernod Flip**—Pernod is a sweetened anise liqueur that mimics the taste of absinthe. Using it in a dessert drink really emphasizes the sweet, candy-like flavors of Pernod.

> 2 oz. Pernod
> 1 oz. half-and-half
> 1 whole egg
> 1 oz. orgeat syrup
> grated nutmeg, to garnish

Combine all ingredients except nutmeg in a blender with ice. Blend until smooth and pour into a sour glass. Garnish with nutmeg.

**Port Wine Flip**—Try the master recipe using a ruby port in place of the brandy. Alternatively, a cream sherry makes a fabulous flip.

**Sloe Gin Flip**—An oldie but a goodie. Sloe gin makes adding fruity flavors to a dessert drink easy. It can be mixed with dairy without causing curdling, which means this flip can be made the classic way, by shaking.

> 2 oz. sloe gin
> 1 oz. half-and-half
> 1 whole egg
> ½ tsp. sugar
> grated nutmeg, to garnish

Combine all ingredients except nutmeg in a shaker with ice. Shake to chill and strain out the ice. Return the liquid to the shaker and shake again (dry shake) for body and pour into a small white wine glass. Sprinkle with nutmeg.

**Strega Flip**—This unusual blended flip uses an herbal Alpine spirit and brandy as well as a lot of lemon juice, which sets it apart from other flips. It's also bigger and necessitates a highball glass.

> 2 oz. Strega
> 1 oz. brandy
> ½ oz. simple syrup
> 1 whole egg
> 1 oz. lemon juice
> grated nutmeg, to garnish

Combine all ingredients in the order written (except nutmeg) in a blender with ice. Blend until smooth and pour into a chilled highball glass. Sprinkle nutmeg on top

## "Shake It, Shake It, Baby!"

Colonial dessert cocktails weren't shaken because the cocktail shaker hadn't yet come into being. Milk punches and eggnogs were mostly served in large quantities, and the milk used came directly from the cows and would produce a fatty froth on top of the bowl when it was whipped. These kinds of drinks were only served in the winter when they could be chilled outside.

Ice was scarce in those days as well, and better suited to cooling fruit than chilling a cocktail, given its impurities and lack of clarity. No one from the colonial world would have considered drinking a cocktail served on the rocks, and blending, of course, was impossible. But once clarified ice and shaker tins became modern conveniences, bartenders used them to their advantage in making single-serving cocktails with a rich froth on top.

The trick to shaking egg cocktails involves two shakes, actually. First fill the shaker with all the ingredients but no ice—spirits, egg, dairy, and sugar—and do what is called a "dry shake." Think "dry run," (not lacking moisture) because this first shake aerates and combines ingredients while breaking up the egg yolk and white. Remember to shake vigorously and hold tightly to both ends of the shaker; the expanding foam in the shaker tends to push your seal apart, and you don't want it to pop open mid-shake.

After about a half-minute of hard shaking, open the tin and add ice before shaking again for a briefer duration. This second shake chills the ingredients before you strain into your glass. It's not necessary to do a third shake without the ice that is done with some fizzes because there is no (or very little) citrus juice in a flip. A Ramos fizz, for instance, needs a final shake without ice to create firm bubbles of half-and-half, egg white protein, sugar, and citrus when soda is added. A flip only needs to be frothy on top, so strain directly into the glass from the shaker tin.

# Eggnog

 Nogs follow a similar prescription to flips, usually calling for more milk. They are the "long" version of the flip, and like flips, they can be made with brandy, dark rum, port, cream sherry, and whiskey.

**Eggnog** (for a party of twenty-five)—Colonial eggnogs were not made in single servings, but served in punch bowls. This large recipe requires whipping the ingredients in the bowl in which it will be served.

> 1 bottle (750 ml) brandy
> 1½ quarts of milk
> 1 pint heavy cream, whipped
> 1 cup sugar
> 12 whole eggs
> grated nutmeg, to garnish

Separate the egg yolks from the whites and beat the yolks in a large punch bowl with sugar to combine. Stir in milk and whipped cream and add brandy. Refrigerate for at least an hour. Before serving, whip the egg whites stiff and fold into the eggnog.

**Baltimore Eggnog**—This deluxe eggnog recipe is a single serving honoring England's Lord Baltimore.

> 2 oz. brandy (cognac please)
> 1 oz. dark rum
> 1 oz. Madeira
> 6 oz. half-and-half
> 1 whole egg
> 1 tsp. sugar
> grated nutmeg, to garnish

Combine all ingredients except nutmeg in a shaker with ice. Shake and strain into a Collins glass and sprinkle nutmeg on top.

**Coffee Eggnog**—Unlike the coffee flip, this cocktail has instant coffee in the mix to make it taste milkier. Whiskey and Kahlua are a great combination, but try gold rum or gold tequila as well.

> 2 oz. blended whiskey
> 1 oz. coffee liqueur
> 6 oz. milk
> 1 oz. half-and-half
> 1 tsp. simple syrup
> ½ tsp. instant coffee
> 1 whole egg
> grated nutmeg, to garnish

Combine all ingredients except nutmeg in a blender with ice. Blend until smooth and pour into a chilled Collins glass. Sprinkle nutmeg on top.

**General Harrison's Eggnog**—Not a big drinker, that general. He preferred his eggnog made with cider, either alcoholic or non-alcoholic. This is a fresh (and, if alcoholic) fizzy eggnog like none other.

> 1 egg
> 1 tsp. sugar
> hard or flat cider, to top
> grated nutmeg, to garnish

Combine egg and sugar in a shaker with ice. Shake and strain into a chilled Collins glass. Fill with hard or flat cider and grate nutmeg on top.

# My Eggnog Recipe

_____

_____

_____

_____

_____

_____

_____

_____

# My Flip Recipe

_____

_____

_____

_____

_____

_____

_____

_____

# Dessert Drinks

 Modern spirits have made many dessert cocktails possible that our colonial forebears could never dream of. The following are dessert drinks and nightcaps that help keep the party going after dinner.

**Banana Milkshake**—There's no reason not to make this drink in a sippy cup. No...no. None that I can imagine.

> 2 oz. light rum
> 1 oz. crème de bananes
> 2 oz. half-and-half
> 1 dash grenadine
> ground nutmeg and banana slice, to garnish

Combine grenadine, half-and-half, and spirits in a shaker with ice. Shake and strain into a chilled cocktail glass. Garnish with the banana slice, and dust with nutmeg.

**Brandy Alexander**—The modern rendition of the flip using dark crème de cacao to add chocolate to an already great cocktail. (To make the original Alexander, use gin in place of brandy. Alexander's Sister substitutes crème de menthe for the crème de cacao.)

> 1½ oz. brandy
> 1½ oz. dark crème de cacao
> 1½ oz. half-and-half
> grated nutmeg, to garnish

Combine liquid ingredients in a shaker with ice. Shake and strain into a chilled cocktail glass. Sprinkle nutmeg on top.

**Coffee Cocktail**—This cocktail has a misleading name. It was intended to be enjoyed while sipping coffee. It has all the components of a port flip with the honeyed deliciousness of yellow Chartreuse and grated chocolate. If you like green Chartreuse and are on the fence about adding the yellow to your collection, this cocktail is reason enough to do just that.

> 3 oz. ruby port
> 1 oz. yellow Chartreuse
> 1 egg yolk
> grated semi-sweet chocolate, to garnish

Combine all ingredients except chocolate in a blender with ice. Blend until smooth and pour into a wine goblet. Grate chocolate on top.

**Golden Cadillac**—Galliano is an Italian sweet liqueur that is flavored with vanilla and anise seeds for a rich and strong dessert drink. If you don't already have Galliano on your bar for Harvey Wallbangers, this drink might persuade you to change that.

> 2 oz. Galliano
> 1 oz. half-and-half
> 1 oz. crème de cacao

Combine all ingredients in a shaker with ice. Shake and strain into a chilled cocktail glass.

**Grasshopper**—The iconic bright green dessert drink so popular in the 1960s that needs to be rediscovered.

> 2 oz. green crème de menthe
> 2 oz. white crème de cacao
> 2 oz. half-and-half

Combine all ingredients in a shaker with ice. Shake and strain into a chilled cocktail glass.

**Good and Plenty**—A blended ice cream cocktail that almost tastes like the candy of the same name but much creamier.

> 1 oz. vodka
> 1 oz. Kahlua coffee liqueur
> ½ scoop vanilla ice cream
> 1 dash Pernod

Combine all ingredients in a blender and blend for three seconds. Pour into a wine glass.

**Ich Bin**—It's an apple brandy flip with a hint of orange from the curaçao.

> 2 oz. apple brandy
> ½ oz. (white) curaçao
> 2 oz. half-and-half
> 1 egg yolk
> grated nutmeg, to garnish

Combine all ingredients except nutmeg in a blender with cracked ice. Blend until smooth and fluffy, and pour into a chilled sour glass. Sprinkle nutmeg on top.

**Milk Punch**—This is a single serving cocktail that works with both gin and whiskey. Of course, it is completely possible to multiply the ingredients by the number of servings you wish to make and serve it in a punch bowl after an hour of refrigerating.

> 3 oz. gin or whiskey
> 8 oz. milk
> 1 tsp. simple syrup
> grated nutmeg, to garnish

Combine all ingredients except nutmeg in a shaker with ice. Shake and strain into a Collins glass full of fresh ice. Dust with nutmeg.

**Olé**—There had to be at least one dessert drink with tequila.

> 2 oz. silver tequila
> 1 oz. coffee liqueur
> 1 tsp. simple syrup
> ½ oz. half-and-half

Combine all ingredients in a shaker with ice. Shake and strain into a chilled cocktail glass.

**Ocho Rios**—Jamaican rums lend themselves perfectly to dessert drinks with their rich molasses flavors. Falernum is a sweet, spiced rum liqueur that adds a tropical flavor to drinks. John D. Taylor's Velvet Falernum is the most widely available brand. If you don't have it, substitute with a spiced rum. When adding these ingredients into the blender, put the half-and-half in last.

> 2 oz. dark rum
> 1 oz. guava nectar
> 1 oz. lime juice
> 1 tsp. falernum
> 1 oz. half-and-half

Combine all ingredients in a blender with ice. Blend until smooth and pour into a champagne flute.

**Pink Squirrel**—The bright red almond flavored crème de noyaux isn't a requirement for every bar, but this cocktail makes an excellent case for having it.

> 2 oz. half-and-half
> 1 oz. crème de cacao
> 1 oz. crème de noyaux (I recommend Tempus Fugit)

Combine all ingredients in a shaker with ice. Shake and strain into a chilled cocktail glass.

**Scotch and Milk**—It's a nightcap more than a dessert with equal parts (you guessed it) scotch and 2% milk poured over ice in an old-fashioned glass. Try with rich blends like Dewar's 12-year-old or Teacher's Highland Cream.

**Russian Quaalude**—Obviously, a modern cocktail making use of popular liqueurs that hit the market in the latter half of the twentieth century. Not bad for a dessert drink. Think a nutty White Russian.

> 2 oz. vodka
> 1 oz. Frangelico
> 1 oz. Bailey's Irish Cream liqueur

Combine all ingredients in a shaker with ice. Shake and strain into a chilled old-fashioned glass.

**White Russian**—Every group of friends has a White Russian drinker. If you don't know who that is, it might be you.

> 2 oz. vodka
> 1 oz. heavy cream
> 1 oz. coffee liqueur

Combine all ingredients in a shaker with ice. Shake and pour into an old-fashioned glass.

# My Dessert Cocktail Recipe

_____

_____

_____

_____

_____

_____

_____

_____

# THE MANHATTAN PROJECT

I'm often asked what cocktail I most enjoy making for someone else. While I have no favorite cocktail for drinking, I always like making a Manhattan for whiskey connoisseurs. There is something of a ritual in selecting the whiskey and watching their eyes light up when I dash the bitters and drizzle the vermouth into the mixing glass and stir it with ice. It is a pleasure for me because Manhattan drinkers—a less picky breed than martini drinkers—are eager to try the bartender's recommendations. They are more concerned with the quality of the spirits than they are about the proportions or modifications to the recipe.

And that, I think, is because the Manhattan is probably the most forgiving of all cocktails served up. There is no acidity or sugar to balance. Each ingredient does its part to a greater or lesser extent depending on the brand and the quantity you choose, but the result is almost always a satisfied customer. That doesn't mean that you can't create a wonderous variety of flavors in Manhattans, but it does mean that if you are among the many lovers of this cocktail, you are certain to find your favorite recipe after a few experiments.

# Manhattans

## Manhattan Master Recipe

The Manhattan is a simple three-ingredient recipe.

**2–3 oz. rye whiskey (Redemption Rye or Dad's Hat are quality choices)**
**½ oz. Italian (sweet) vermouth**
**1 dash Angostura bitters**
**maraschino cherry, to garnish**

Stir all liquid ingredients in a mixing glass with ice and strain into a chilled cocktail glass. Garnish with the cherry.

## Modifications

Manhattan modifications usually involve substituting the style of whiskey or vermouth. In the case where an additional ingredient is added, it is a good idea to keep the proportions small so as not to stray too far from the original formula. No Manhattan drinker wants their favorite cocktail morphed into a fruity or fizzy monstrosity that only faintly tastes of whiskey. So, you can add sugar, sweet liqueurs, or try a small portion of an Italian amaro or French aromatized wine like Dubonnet Rouge, but no juice, please!

**Adonis**—For a low-ABV Manhattan, try the Adonis made with sherry instead of whiskey. It is about the strength of a glass of wine but half the volume. Make sure to use a richer sherry like Amontillado. A cream sherry will also work but it will be sweeter.

> 3 oz. Amontillado sherry
> 1 oz. Italian (sweet) vermouth
> 1 dash orange bitters
> orange peel, to garnish

Combine ingredients in a mixing glass with ice. Stir and strain into a chilled cocktail glass. Garnish with orange peel

**Bobby Burns**—Named after Scotland's poet, this Manhattan is rich with scotch maltiness and the herbal and honeyed flavors of Bénédictine liqueur.

> 2 oz. scotch
> 1 oz. Italian (sweet) vermouth
> 1 tsp. Bénédictine
> lemon twist, to garnish

Combine all ingredients in a mixing glass with ice and stir. Strain into a chilled cocktail glass and garnish with the lemon twist.

**Boulevardier**—This is the whiskey version of the Negroni for those Manhattan drinkers that can't seem to make it taste bitter enough.

> 1 oz. bourbon (I recommend Jim Beam white label)
> 1 oz. Italian (sweet) vermouth
> 1 oz. Campari
> orange twist, to garnish

Stir liquid ingredients in a mixing glass with ice. Strain into an old-fashioned glass full of fresh ice or a single large cube. Twist the orange zest over the glass and drop it in.

**Bonaparte's Manhattan**—Add ¾ oz. of French mandarin liqueur, Mandarine Napoléon, to the master recipe and substitute orange bitters for the Angostura bitters.

**Brandy Manhattan**—Substitute cognac or American brandy for the whiskey in the master recipe.

**Brooklyn Cocktail**—The brother to the Manhattan, the Brooklyn requires maraschino liqueur and a very rare orange bitter, Amer Picon, to set it apart from its neighboring borough.

> ½ oz. rye whiskey
> ½ oz. French (dry) vermouth
> ¼ oz. Luxardo Maraschino liqueur
> ¼ oz. Amer Picon (Amaro Meletti or Amaro Ramazzotti
>    make good substitutes)

Combine all ingredients in a mixing glass with ice and stir. Strain into a chilled cocktail glass.

**Delmonico Cocktail**—A classic gin and brandy cocktail that straddles the Manhattan and martini worlds well.

> 1½ oz. gin (London dry gin like Beefeater)
> 1 oz. brandy (German brandy like Asbach Uralt)
> ½ oz. French (dry) vermouth
> ½ oz. Italian (sweet) vermouth
> 2 dashes Angostura bitters
> lemon twist, to garnish

Combine all liquid ingredients in a mixing glass with ice. Stir and strain into a chilled cocktail glass. Garnish with a lemon twist.

**Dutch Manhattan**—Genever is a Dutch spirit that is something of a cross between gin and whiskey. Aged genever like Bols Barrel Aged brand is very smooth and malty with hints of juniper and oak. For this variation, substitute Bols Barrel Aged genever for the rye in the master recipe.

**Dry Manhattan**—The original Manhattan recipe is very flavorful and rich. It's a winter drink, for sure, and all the richness in the vermouth tends to cover over the flavor of the whiskey. The idea behind the dry Manhattan is to make a whiskey-forward cocktail that is lighter on sugar and brighter in color.

> 2–3 oz. rye whiskey
> ½ oz. French (dry) vermouth (like Dolin Extra Dry)
> 1 dash orange bitters
> lemon twist, to garnish

Stir all liquid ingredients in a mixing glass with ice and strain into a chilled cocktail glass. Garnish with the lemon twist

**Paddy Cocktail**—Substitute Irish Whiskey for the rye in the master recipe.

**Perfect Manhattan**—add ½ oz. of French (dry) vermouth to the master recipe.

**Rob Roy**—Scotland's famous outlaw makes an appearance among these Manhattan recipes. A single malt can be a bit overbearing in this recipe, so stick to your favorite blend. Cutty Sark Prohibition Edition scotch is especially good with its light caramel and malt notes.

> 2 oz. scotch (use Cutty Sark Prohibition Edition)
> ½ oz. Italian (sweet) vermouth
> several dashes of orange bitters
> maraschino cherry, to garnish

Combine all liquid ingredients with ice in a mixing glass and stir. Strain into a chilled cocktail glass and garnish with a cherry.

## "So.... What Is Vermouth, Exactly?"

Vermouth is a type of aromatized and bitter wine that originated in central and southern Europe. It comes in many varieties, but the main ones are dry and sweet.

Dry vermouth is exactly what it sounds like—mouth-puckeringly dry with sharp herbal notes and sometimes hints of apricot or pear. Recipes in this book refer to dry vermouth as French because French vintners developed this style that became famous as the essential ingredient in a martini. Look to the French brands like Dolin's Extra Dry and Noilly Prat for a good dry vermouth.

Sweet vermouth, by contrast, is an Italian invention. It is also bitter, but has a sweet and thick texture because caramel is folded into it. This is the critical ingredient that gives the Manhattan its balance of sweet caramel and woody bitterness. Carpano Antica Formula Sweet Vermouth is perhaps the most intense sweet vermouth, but Martini & Rossi Sweet Vermouth is widely available.

Interesting Fact! Both sweet and dry vermouths are made from white wine. It is the caramel that gives sweet vermouth its amber color.

---

**Sombrero**—Try making the Manhattan master recipe with añejo tequila. Don Julio Añejo is recommended.

**Sweet Manhattan**—Increase the proportion of sweet vermouth in the master recipe to at least 1 oz. A 50/50 Manhattan is what you get when the sweet vermouth proportion equals the amount of whiskey. An "upside-down Manhattan" is when the proportion of vermouth exceeds the whiskey proportion.

**Swiss Manhattan**—Kirschwasser is a crystal clear, Black Forest cherry brandy that has a fruity scent and a fiery alcohol content. This Manhattan variation is very dry with an enticing nose similar to chocolate-covered cherries.

> 1½ oz. bourbon
> 1½ oz. crème de cacao or chocolate spirit
> ½ oz. French (dry) vermouth
> ½ oz. kirschwasser
> several dashes aromatic bitters
> maraschino cherry, to garnish

Stir all liquid ingredients in a mixing glass with ice and strain into a chilled cocktail glass. Garnish with the cherry.

## My Manhattan Recipe

_____

_____

_____

_____

_____

_____

_____

_____

_____

# WHAT MAKES A MARTINI
# A MARTINI?

It's perhaps the most recognizable cocktail in the world. James Bond orders one to exact specifications in every 007 film. Neon billboards depicting a triangular glass and a round garnish light up around the world to indicate a cocktail bar or lounge is nearby. Its silhouette is splashed notoriously in the logos of anti-drunk driving organizations. Type cocktail into your smartphone and a martini emoji appears. The martini, for better or worse, has become synonymous with the word cocktail. With all of this notoriety, it is fair to say that the martini is the world's most beloved and hated cocktail of all time.

The much-maligned martini could be a victim of its own popularity. Most of the animosity toward the drink is undoubtedly borne from confusion about its ingredients. Is any drink in an angular cocktail glass considered a martini? That depends on who you ask.

In the 1990s, it wasn't uncommon to see entire martini menus featuring all the colors of the rainbow plus chocolate, coffee, and Irish cream varieties. For this reason, bartenders stifle a sigh when a guest orders a martini, prompting numerous clarifying questions: Vodka or gin? Up or on the rocks? Dry, wet, or dirty? Olive or a twist? Often it turns out that the martini drinker simply wants a generous helping of chilled vodka. What is the home bartender supposed to make of all of this?

Fortunately, classic cocktail books provide us insight into the intention of the drink. Whatever the cocktail's origin, be it the purported gold miners in San Francisco or glitzy New York hotels trying to sell the new Martini & Rossi vermouth, the original martini was always a vermouth drink. Vermouth was a popular libation at the end of the nineteenth century. The introduction of gin (vodka wasn't consumed outside of Russia at this time) was really a method of increasing the potency of a glass of vermouth. Once Prohibition made vermouth scarce, the martini became a necessary prescription for scofflaws in speakeasies. Bootleg bathtub gin was used to spread out the vermouth; and the vermouth, in turn, covered up the unpleasant flavors of poor-quality spirits. Pickled and acidic garnishes such as olives also made the harsh liquors more palatable.

For bartenders, it's helpful to have a standard to refer to when making martinis for the first time. A true martini is a chilled, clear spirit cocktail with some quantity of vermouth. Notice I didn't say it had to be gin. I love vodka martinis and even Bacardi rum martinis if they are done well, which means no fruit juice, sugar, or dairy, please. For the purposes of this book, I will cover classic martini recipes and other spirits-only cocktails that martini drinkers will appreciate.

# Martinis

## Martini Master Recipe

 Of course, the original martini was made with gin, but vodka is completely acceptable if that's your taste. For a vodka martini, I recommend a flavorful brand like Grey Goose with its hint of citrus from French wheat. Stirring is a requirement for the master recipe, but, again, that is a matter of taste.

> 3 oz. dry gin or premium vodka
> ½ oz. French (dry) vermouth
> olive on a cocktail pick or a lemon twist, to garnish

Stir liquid ingredients with plenty of ice in a mixing glass. Strain into a chilled cocktail (martini) glass and garnish according to preference.

## Modifications

Most of the adjustments made to martinis come in the form of the proportion of spirit to vermouth or choice of garnish. Cocktail onions like in the Gibson, or a black olive in the Buckeye martini create such wholly different flavor experiences that they need to be tried out at least once. Drinkers who like their brine will, of course, find the dirty martini is their favorite, and the dill martini will satisfy the pickle lovers. If you like French (dry) vermouth and prefer your drinks less potent, I recommend the 50/50 martini with equal parts spirit and vermouth.

**007 Martini**—This is the martini that James Bond orders so often. Also known as the Vesper, and the James Bond, this version includes both gin and vodka and Lillet Blanc, a sweet wine aperitif flavored with bitter oranges. Feel free to play with the proportion of gin to vodka, but by all means, make sure it is "shaken not stirred."

> 2 oz. gin
> 1 oz. vodka
> ½ oz. Lillet Blanc
> lemon twist, to garnish

Combine all spirits in a shaker with ice and shake vigorously. Double strain into a chilled cocktail (martini) glass, and twist the lemon zest over the drink before dropping it in.

**50/50 Martini**—This is the vermouth-heavy, pre-prohibition martini recipe mentioned above. Instead of a spirits heavy drink, it is now equal parts French (dry) vermouth and your choice of gin or vodka.

**Apple Martini**—I feel that this recipe is borderline martini at best. When it appeared in bars in the 1990s, it opened up a whole range of colorful cocktails based on the martini and is served in a cocktail glass. With a small portion of dry vermouth in it, I can accept it as part of the martini family. Feel free to shake or stir according to preference.

> 2 oz. vodka
> 1 oz. Apple Pucker liqueur
> ¼ oz. French (dry) vermouth
> maraschino cherry, to garnish

Shake or stir ingredients with ice. Double strain into a chilled cocktail (martini) glass and garnish with the cherry.

## "Shake, Stir.... What's the Difference?"

Some martini purists will say that a martini should only be stirred and that shaking "bruises" the gin, whatever that means. What it comes down to is that shaking a cocktail aerates the liquid, stirring up lots of bubbles and chipping off pieces of ice that the strainer cannot catch. This is fine when making a juicy cocktail—perhaps one that is not served up but strained into a glass with ice. (Egg white cocktails demand a good shake to create foam, for instance.) In that case, shaking is designed to chill the cocktail quickly. But when your spirits are clear, as they are in a standard martini, they will come out of a shaker opaque with bubbles and full of ice chips that float on top and eventually melt. This adds more dilution than some drinkers would like. So, while shaking is a good way to chill a drink quickly, it's not the prettiest way to make a martini.

A good rule of thumb for chilling all cocktails is to shake when there is juice and sugar in the drink and to stir when there is only wine and/or spirits. This doesn't always hold true, if you read ahead to some of the recipes involving liqueurs and colored spirits. But in every case where a cocktail is shaken and served up or neat, make sure to use a cone strainer to double strain out the ice chunks.

Finally, shaking or stirring really depends on personal preference. Just ask James Bond, who insists on violently shaking his gin and vodka for symbolism or something. Maybe he likes having a diluted drink to help keep his wits about him.

**Blue Sapphire Martini**—This cocktail produces an aesthetically pleasing blue shade to match the bottle of Bombay Sapphire.

> 3 oz. Bombay Sapphire gin
> ½ oz. French (dry) vermouth
> ¼ oz. blue curaçao
> lemon twist, to garnish

Shake on ice and double strain into a cocktail glass. Twist lemon zest over the glass, and drop it in the drink.

**Carmen Cavallaro**—This is the famous pianist known for his light piano soloist style. It is a rich and bodacious portion of a martini. Sherry and oak notes are the stars of this cocktail with just a hint of orange from the curacao.

> 2 oz. gin (Bluecoat Barrel Reserve gin recommended)
> 3/4 oz. fino (dry) sherry
> 3/4 oz. French (dry) vermouth
> dash curacao

Combine all ingredients in a mixing glass with ice and stir. Strain into a chilled cocktail glass while listening to piano music.

**Cool Yule Martini**—This odd martini variation is really a strange departure from the master recipe and might not appeal to the avid martini drinker. Still, it is worth trying during the holiday season because of the candy cane garnish and the chilling effect of peppermint schnapps.

> 3 oz. vodka (I suggest Stolichnaya)
> ½ oz. French (dry) vermouth (like Noilly Prat)
> 1 tsp. peppermint schnapps
> 1 candy cane, to garnish

Shake liquid ingredients in a shaker with ice. Double strain into a chilled cocktail glass. Garnish with candy cane.

**Dill Martini**—That angular glass sometimes needs an eye-catching garnish. Someone who sticks a pickled cucumber spear in their martini might be craving attention from bar guests, but the brine of a pickle is very different than the flavor that an olive lends to your spirit. Try it and judge for yourself.

> 2½ oz. vodka (I suggest Stolichnaya)
> ½ oz. French (dry) vermouth (like Noilly Prat)
> Dill pickle, to garnish

Combine liquid ingredients in a mixing glass with ice. Stir and strain into a chilled cocktail glass. Garnish with dill pickle spear.

**Dirty Martini**—The depths of depravity that martini drinkers eventually succumb to include putting a lot of olive brine in your cocktail. Then again, some people really like the taste of olives and use it to flavor their spirits. Olive juice is also loaded with salt and electrolytes that might abate a bad hangover, so there might be some logic to this strange recipe.

> 3 oz. of gin or vodka (I prefer gin for a richer flavor)
> ½ oz. French (dry) vermouth (optional)
> ½–2 oz. olive brine from the jar
> As many olives you can fit on a cocktail sword, to garnish

Combine all liquid ingredients in a shaker with ice. Shake and strain (dirty, no cone strainer) into a cocktail glass. Garnish with at least three olives.

**Gibson**—garnish your vodka or gin martini with those sweet and tangy cocktail onions on a cocktail pic for an interesting flavor experience.

**Mariner Martini**—For those who really love anchovies, make with olives hand-stuffed with anchovies. The oils and salt from the anchovies really send the flavors of this cocktail in a seaward direction. Another suggestion is to substitute the dry vermouth with several dashes of white vinegar infused with anchovy oil.

**Martinez**—The originator of the martini, according to some. It gets its name from the Nouthern California town where it was first made for a gold miner who was celebrating a promising load.

> 1½ oz. Old Tom gin (I prefer Hayman's)
> 1½ oz. Italian (sweet) vermouth
> ¼ oz. Luxardo Maraschino liqueur
> 2 dashes Angostura bitters
> orange twist, to garnish

Combine all liquid ingredients in a mixing glass with ice. Stir and strain into a chilled cocktail glass. Garnish with an orange twist.

**Muscovy Martini**—Substitute the vermouth in the master recipe with kümmel, an Eastern European caraway and honey spirit. Use a black olive for the garnish.

**Naked Martini**—When making the master recipe, pour vermouth over ice in the mixing glass, swirl and discard the vermouth. This coats the ice with just a kiss of vermouth before you add your spirit.

**Negroni**—The bitterest martini with the sweet vermouth. Campari is an Italian aperitif spirit with a brilliant red color and bitter taste. If you are looking to expand your taste horizons, this cocktail will challenge you.

>  1 oz. gin
>  1 oz. Italian (sweet) vermouth
>  1 oz. Campari
>  orange twist, to garnish

Combine all ingredients in a mixing glass with ice. Stir and strain into a chilled coupe and garnish with an orange twist.

Alternative serving suggestion: Strain into an old-fashioned glass with a large ice cube and squeeze the orange twist over top before dropping it in the drink.

**Newbury**—A relative of the martini that swings a little sweet. For that reason, I recommend a particularly malty and funky gin to balance the orange flavor of triple sec.

>  2 oz. gin (try it with Ransom Old Tom)
>  1½ oz. Italian (sweet) vermouth
>  1 dash triple sec (try it with Cointreau)
>  lemon twist, to garnish

Combine all liquid ingredients in a shaker with ice. Shake and strain into a chilled cocktail glass. Squeeze the twist over the glass and drop it in.

**Paisley Martini**—One of several martinis designed to appeal to Scotch drinkers. It's the best of both worlds, as you get the stylish glass and presentation of a martini with the added richness of scotch. Of course, the selection of scotch makes a big difference. A big blend brand like Johnny Walker will do for a well-rounded scotch flavor with a hint of smoke. Use an Islay single malt like Laphroaig if you want the smoke to dominate the flavor.

> 3 oz. gin
> ½ oz. French (dry) vermouth
> 1 tsp. scotch
> lemon twist, to garnish

Combine gin and vermouth in a shaker with ice. Shake and double strain into a chilled cocktail glass. Float scotch on top and garnish with lemon twist.

**Perfect Martini**—Make the master recipe with your choice of spirit and garnish, but only include a half teaspoon each of sweet and dry vermouth.

**Russian Rob Roy**—Vodka has the ability to thin the heaviness of scotch without lowering the alcohol content. The effect is a much lighter tasting Rob Roy.

> 2 oz. vodka
> ½ oz. scotch
> ½ oz. French (dry) vermouth.
> lemon twist, to garnish

Stir all ingredients in a mixing glass with ice. Strain into a chilled cocktail glass and garnish with a lemon twist.

**Soviet Cocktail**—Manzanilla sherry is dry and very aromatic, but not spiced like vermouth. The effect is a liquid with a silky body that complements a good Russian vodka.

> 3 oz. Stolichnaya vodka
> 1 oz. Manzanilla sherry
> ½ oz. French (dry) vermouth
> lemon twist, to garnish

Stir all ingredients in a mixing glass with ice and strain into a chilled cocktail glass. Garnish with lemon twist.

**St. Petersburg**—A vodka lover's dream. Orange bitters and an orange slice make each sip intensely fruity and spicy.

> 3 oz. vodka
> ½ tsp. orange bitters
> orange slice, to garnish
> Put vodka and bitters in an old-fashioned glass full of ice.
> Stir to chill and garnish with a slice of orange.

**Tuxedo**—This cousin of the martini goes for bitter and sweet liqueurs that come together in a fresh and classy union. This is a good one to try if you are getting bored with the master recipe.

> 1 oz. French (dry) vermouth
> 1 oz. gin (I recommend Hayman's Old Tom)
> ½ tsp. Luxardo Maraschino liqueur
> 1 dash absinthe
> 3 dashes orange bitters
> lemon twist and maraschino cherry, to garnish

Combine all ingredients in a mixing glass and stir to chill. Strain into a chilled cocktail glass. Garnish with fruit.

# My Martini Recipe

_____

_____

_____

_____

_____

_____

_____

_____

_____

# "I'LL HAVE AN OLD-FASHIONED."

The classic old-fashioned phrase I chose for this chapter is spoken dozens of times a day in bars all over the world. This great grandfather of cocktails went from relative obscurity to a daily ritual enjoyed in twenty-first-century watering holes as well as living rooms. It's hard to overstate the popularity of the old-fashioned in the bar scene today.

I credit the television series *Mad Men* for bringing the old-fashioned back into vogue. While there may not be a direct correlation, I always ended up making more old-fashioneds on Thursday nights when the show was airing than I would the rest of the week. It mystified me how nonchalantly guests said the exact words, "I'll have an old-fashioned" as if there was nothing unusual about their request or the fact that about a hundred people before them said the same five words in precisely the same way.

The universal popularity of the old-fashioned means it cannot be ignored on your home bar menu. Certainly, as a home bartender, you have your favorite methods and spirits for making an old-fashioned to your liking, but it is critical to keep in mind that the name "old-fashioned" means different things to different people depending on their age and where they are from.

That is because the recipe has morphed into variations involving more or less fruit and sugar as it spread across the United States, like a sentence in a game of telephone. In some parts of the Midwest, the old-fashioned has become a fizzy tropical drink that bears little resemblance to the stripped-down master recipe below. I'm fine with a Wisconsin old-fashioned when I know what I'm ordering, but I'm betting a New Yorker would scoff at the muddled cherries and orange slices in the glass and hand it back to you. Even I have drawn a line and rejected an old-fashioned with a grapefruit wedge smashed into a fruit salad of a drink. If I can't taste the whiskey, the recipe won't work for me.

As a home bartender, you know your guests, but you might not know their preferences. Feel free to ask and involve them in the preparation: "Do you like muddled cherries in your drink?" for instance. Being attentive to your guest's tastes will make for a better experience and will help you make and keep friends.

# Old-Fashioneds

## Old-Fashioned Master Recipe

 The master recipe should reflect the majority of recipes for old-fashioned as I've seen them done. I like that the drink is prepared and served in a glass bearing its name.

2 oz. American whiskey (I recommend Jim Beam
    Black Label bourbon)
1 tsp. Sugar in the Raw or demerara sugar
1 splash filtered water
2 dashes Angostura bitters
orange twist, to garnish

In an old-fashioned glass, add sugar, water, and bitters, and stir to dissolve the sugar. Add ice and whiskey and stir gently. Twist the orange zest over the drink, and rub it around the edges of the glass before dropping it in.

## Modifications

There are more ways to make an old-fashioned than there are recipes in this entire book, but most variations involve preparation: Do you muddle a sugar cube and fruit? Do you serve the drink with ice or neat? And do you use a sugar syrup instead of granulated sugar? My recommendation is to try doing it several ways and decide for yourself. A mixing glass is not required, which may have helped the drink gain acceptance in casual bars that never bothered equipping staff with mixing glasses. That means it is served with ice, but you may like using a mixing glass and straining your old-fashioned neat. I find that a thick demerara sugar syrup adds sweetness without diluting the drink with the splash of water. But many drinkers like how water softens the whiskey. My only contention is that an old-fashioned is a spirits-for-ward cocktail with sugar and essence of fruit. The focus should be on the whiskey; you should be able to taste it. If there is too much citric acid from fruit juice or too much sweetness that the drink doesn't taste strong, then it's not an old-fashioned.

**Brandy Old-Fashioned**—Substitute an American brandy like Korbel for the whiskey in the master recipe, or try brandy as the principal spirit in the Wisconsin old-fashioned and see which you like better.

**French Connection**—A cognac-based old-fashioned that uses amaretto to sweeten and add a nutty flavor to the mix.

> 1½ oz. cognac
> ¾ oz. amaretto

Combine ingredients in a mixing glass with ice. Stir and strain into a chilled old-fashioned glass full of fresh ice.

**Kentucky Colonel**—Bénédictine, a French herbal spirit made from brandy, both sweetens and flavors the whiskey in this southern sipper.

> 2½ oz. bourbon
> 1 oz. Bénédictine
> lemon twist, to garnish

Combine spirits in a mixing glass with ice and stir. Strain into a chilled cocktail glass and garnish with the lemon twist. This drink can alternatively be served in an old-fashioned glass with no ice to appease the old-fashioned purist.

**Mint Julep**—There's nothing like a mint julep on a summer day. The classic mint julep came about in the early 1800s and rose to fame at the Willard Hotel in Washington, DC, before it became the unofficial drink of the Kentucky Derby. The presentation of the cocktail—in its metal julep cup full of crushed ice—may seem a far cry from the traditional old-fashioned, but the core ingredients are all present and perfect for hot-weather drinking.

> 3 oz. bourbon (I recommend Evan Williams Single Barrel)
> ½ oz. simple syrup
> 10–15 mint leaves
> mint sprig, to garnish

Muddle simple syrup and mint leaves in a metal julep cup or a highball glass. Add whiskey and crushed ice and stir, topping up with more crushed ice to the level of the top of the glass. Garnish with the mint sprig.

**Monte Carlo**—Another Bénédictine-enhanced old-fashioned recipe with more of the bitterness you expect from the classic recipe.

> 2 oz. rye (Use Old Overholt or Rittenhouse)
> ½ oz. Bénédictine
> 2 dashes Angostura bitters
> lemon twist, to garnish

Combine liquid ingredients in a mixing glass with ice. Stir to chill and strain into an old-fashioned glass full of fresh ice. Twist lemon zest over the glass and drop it in.

**Rum Old-Fashioned**—Substitute a rich aged rum like Pusser's Navy Rum or Appleton Estate Reserve for whiskey in the master recipe, and use a lime twist in place of the orange twist.

**Sazerac**—Originating from New Orleans, the Sazerac is the Creole cousin of the old-fashioned. It makes use of Peychaud's bitters and absinthe to scent the cocktail and a lemon twist for more brightness and acidity. These substitutions almost completely alter the drink's flavor profile, but the style and even the texture of the drink are largely unchanged from the master recipe.

> 1 tsp. French absinthe
> 2 oz. rye (use Sazerac or Old Overholt)
> ½ tsp. granulated white sugar
> 2 dashes Peychaud's bitters
> 1 tsp. filtered water
> lemon twist, to garnish

Coat the inside of an old-fashioned glass with absinthe and dump out the remainder. In a mixing glass, stir water, sugar, and bitters to dissolve the sugar. Add rye and ice and stir to chill, then strain into the absinthe-coated glass (i.e., serve neat). Twist the lemon zest over the glass, rubbing it on the rim before dropping it inside.

**Stinger**—A classic and refreshing minty drink that works as a dessert or appetizer.

> 2 oz. cognac (like Hennessy VSOP)
> ½ oz. (white) crème de menthe
> 1 tsp. simple syrup
> mint sprig, to garnish (optional)

Shake liquid ingredients with ice in a shaker and strain into an old-fashioned glass full of fresh ice. Garnish with the mint sprig.

## "Just How Old Is the Old-Fashioned?"

It's certainly not as old as the first distilled spirits, though one could argue that anyone who mixed sugar and bitter herbs in booze that just came off a still to make it more palatable must have invented the old-fashioned, whether it was one hundred or a thousand years ago. The truth is that the old-fashioned, like almost all cocktails, is a relatively new invention when compared to the whole of human history. It is almost exclusively an American whiskey cocktail, after all, and that means it is only about as old as the first whiskey distilleries that took root in the original American colonies a little more than two centuries ago. But even that is being generous.

For a drink recipe to gain the level of notoriety that the old-fashioned enjoys, it must have come into being where most cocktail recipes were born not in the lowly inns and taverns of the colonies, but in hustling cities where hotel bars could supply the ingredients to urbane clientele who could spread the word and entice more patrons to try the libation. So perhaps the old-fashioned was invented in the early nineteenth century along with the mint julep, the Rickey, and the whiskey sour, and the bartenders who made it were using the name as a marketing ploy.

The name of the cocktail suggests, however, that even as it was being made, the old-fashioned was recognized for having the quintessential ingredients that Dereck Brown identifies in his book *Spirits, Sugar, Water, Bitters: How the Cocktail Conquered the World*. So, the name may be more of an assertion that the cocktail's preparation is according to "old-fashioned" methods and should not be taken as a statement of age.

**Sunset Gun**—This variation is steeped in American military tradition. The flag is lowered every evening in the Army camp. At the moment the sun crosses the horizon, a cannon is fired to mark the end of the day. Officers, it seems, enjoyed toasting at this time, and this recipe was created to commemorate the practice. This cocktail uses orange liqueur for the citrus flavor and cloves steeped in whiskey for the bitters.

> 4 oz. bourbon, rye, or blended whiskey
> 1 oz. curaçao or triple sec
> 6 cloves
> 2–3 dashes of orange bitters

Combine all ingredients in a mixing glass and refrigerate for one hour before enjoying. A few minutes before sunset, add ice and stir to chill. Double strain into two cocktail glasses (serve up), and toast with a friend. (Serves two.)

**Tequila Old-Fashioned**—Similar to the rum old-fashioned. The recipe really only works with well-aged tequilas. My recommendation is Don Julio Añejo or Corralejo Reposado because of their rich caramel notes on the finish. Experiment with simple syrup rather than a sugar cube if you like, or try agave nectar for the sweetener. And, like the rum old-fashioned, use a lime twist.

**Wisconsin Old-Fashioned**—Perhaps the most misunderstood version of the old-fashioned out there because it is such a departure. It relies on a "fruit salad" effect of sweetness and tartness that goes well with whiskey but doesn't completely cover the whiskey flavor. It has a messy *smash* appearance that is almost the antithesis of an old-fashioned. But since it is one of the best-known recipes in America's central and northern states, you are pretty much guaranteed to find people who prefer their old-fashioneds like they make them up in Wisconsin.

> **2 oz. American whiskey (use Seagram's 7 Crown for best results)**
> **2 orange slices**
> **2 maraschino cherries**
> **1 sugar cube**
> **7 Up or lemon-lime soda**
> **2 dashes Angostura bitters**
> **1 orange slice and 1 maraschino cherry, to garnish**

Build the drink in its namesake glass with a sugar cube, bitters, and a splash of 7 Up, and stir to dissolve the sugar. Add fruit and muddle until slightly pulverized. Add whiskey and ice and stir to chill. Top with more 7 Up and garnish with more fruit.

## My Old-Fashioned Recipe

_____

_____

_____

_____

_____

_____

_____

_____

# ON SOURS
# & SIDECARS

The final selection of recipes belongs to a very old group of cocktails that use citrus juice and sugar to create a balanced drink served up or on the rocks. Originally, the sour was a tangy form of the flip, with a foamy egg white head above sweet, spirituous delicacy in a sour glass. This glass was a short-stemmed wine glass with a fluted top that forced the drinker to sip through the foam to reach the liquid. This recipe evolved as it spread to include liqueurs like amaretto and triple sec and were served in all manner of glassware. Eventually, most cocktails bearing the name "sour" share little resemblance with the frothy drinks from two centuries ago. To illustrate this point, the pisco sour and margarita—two distinctly different sour cocktails, one with egg white and the other with a salt rim—became the grandchildren of the original recipe. But the one thing all sours have in common is that they are strong, flat cocktails with that unmistakable sweet and sour balance.

The sidecar, as the name would suggest, appeared in the roaring, motorized twentieth century and became a symbol of modernity and class. These drinks featured fruit brandies as the main spirit as well as a number of fruity liqueurs that give them an air of liquid candy. The development of crèmes and cordials with bright, fruity flavors allowed for a nearly unlimited number of variations that include The Last Word and Aviation.

Unlike sours, sidecars tend not to have any egg white foam. They are more consistently served up in a coupe or cocktail glass. Some are even mistakenly referred to as martinis even though there is no vermouth in them. The presence of liqueurs in these cocktails dazzle the taste buds and delight the eyes, since many of these sugary spirits are brightly colored. Your guests will be most impressed with these recipes.

# Sours

## Whiskey Sour Master Recipe

Whiskey is probably the most often requested spirit in the original sour. As such, it is critical to choose a whiskey that is mellow and mixable. You could use an Islay single malt scotch, but the point of the sour is to make the spirit as silky and delicious as possible for inexperienced drinkers. When it comes to smoothness, the Irish have the world beat, so my master recipe is the Boston sour made with Jameson.

> 2 oz. Jameson blended Irish whiskey
> 1 tsp. sugar
> 1 oz. lemon juice
> 1 egg white
> maraschino cherry and lemon wheel, to garnish

Combine sugar, whiskey, lemon juice, and egg white in a shaker and shake well until foamy. Add ice and shake again to chill. Strain into a chilled sour glass and garnish with lemon and cherry on a cocktail pick.

## Modifications

Egg white foam isn't for everyone, so it is no surprise that for most bars, this ingredient so subject to spoilage fell by the wayside along with its requisite sour glass. This glass looks like a short wine glass with steep walls to allow the egg white foam to rise to the drinker's nose. The chilled cocktail beneath had no ice. Whiskey sours the world over are now mostly served on the rocks in old-fashioned glasses. (The recipes below that do not call for ice in the glass are made to be served up or in a sour glass, but these can be done "on the rocks" in an old-fashioned glass.) Brandy, rum, vodka, tequila, and gin make for some adventurous variations of the main spirit, while amaretto and other liqueurs make for a sweeter, lower-proof drinking experience.

**Amaretto Sour**—Amaretto is a nutty, cookie-flavored spirit better suited to dessert than a before-dinner cocktail. This cocktail is rich and really draws the drinker in. Very relaxing.

> 2 oz. amaretto
> 1 oz. lemon juice
> orange slice, to garnish

Combine all ingredients except orange slice in a shaker with ice. Shake and strain into a sour or old-fashioned glass. Garnish with orange slice.

**Applejack Sour**—Applejack is sometimes referred to as "apple whiskey." It is really more of a brandy, made with fortified apple cider and sometimes mixed with apple brandy. It tastes like cider and can have a barrel taste similar to whiskey as well.

> 2 oz. applejack
> 1 oz. lemon juice
> ½ oz. simple syrup
> lemon wheel, to garnish

Combine all ingredients except lemon wheel in a shaker with ice. Shake and strain into a chilled cocktail glass. Garnish with a lemon wheel.

**Apricot Sour**—This is when your purchase of apricot flavored brandy will impress your guests. This is a sweet sour, similar to the amaretto sour but with a distinctly summery taste.

> 2 oz. apricot flavored brandy
> 1 oz. lemon juice
> ½ tsp. simple syrup
> lemon slice, to garnish

Combine liquid ingredients in a shaker with ice. Shake and strain into a chilled cocktail (or sour) glass. Garnish with the lemon slice.

**Frisco Sour**—People from San Francisco will remind you not to call their city "Frisco." The thing that stands out in this cocktail is the sweet herbal notes of Bénédictine and its rosy color from grenadine.

> 1½ oz. blended whiskey
> ¾ oz. Bénédictine
> 1 tsp. lemon juice
> 1 tsp. lime juice
> 1 tsp. simple syrup (optional)
> 1 dash grenadine
> orange slice, to garnish

Combine liquid ingredients in a shaker with ice. Shake and strain into a chilled sour glass or white wine glass. Garnish with the orange slice.

**Grafton Street Sour**—Grafton Street is a touristy street in Dublin, Ireland. This cocktail will please most drinkers with the addition of Chambord raspberry liqueur floating on top of the sour mix. The key is to keep the sugar content of the cocktail higher than the Chambord, which, when poured over the back of a bar spoon, will make a purple layer that the drinker will notice on first sip.

> 1 ½ oz. Irish whiskey
> ½ oz. triple sec
> 1 oz. lime juice
> ½ oz. simple syrup
> ¼ oz. Chambord
> lime wheel, to garnish

Combine all liquid ingredients except Chambord in a shaker with ice. Strain into an old-fashioned glass filled with fresh ice. Float the Chambord on top by pouring over the back of a bar spoon and garnish with a lime wheel.

**Los Angeles Cocktail**—Big American cities have to have their cocktails. This lesser known concoction is very rich and high in acidity, which is a nice contrast with the heaviness of egg. Shaking it very vigorously without ice first really helps to incorporate and aerate the ingredients and make for a foamy delight.

> 2 oz. rye whiskey
> 1 oz. lime juice
> ¼ tsp. Italian (sweet) vermouth
> 1 tsp. sugar
> 1 whole egg

Combine all ingredients in a shaker and shake vigorously. Add ice and shake again. Strain into a chilled sour glass.

**New York Cocktail**—Forget the Manhattan, sour drinkers want this tart cocktail.

>   2 oz. blended whiskey
>   1 oz. lemon juice
>   ½ tsp. grenadine
>   1 tsp. simple syrup
>   lemon twist, to garnish

Combine liquid ingredients in a shaker with ice. Shake and strain into a chilled cocktail glass. Garnish with a twist of lemon.

**New York Sour**—When made correctly, it is possible to float a full-bodied red wine like Cabernet or Merlot on top of the sweeter, heavier sour mixture.

>   2 oz. blended whiskey
>   1½ oz. lemon juice
>   1 tsp. simple syrup
>   ½ oz. dry red wine

Combine all ingredients except wine in a shaker with ice. Shake and strain into a sour glass. Gently float the red wine on top by pouring over the back of a bar spoon to distribute the weight.

**Penicillin**—A relatively new arrival in the sour family of cocktails, the penicillin is an outstanding drink that is so memorable you will be craving it several days after you first try it.

> 1½ oz. blended scotch
> ½ oz. ginger liqueur (I recommend Domaine de Canton)
> ⅓ oz. Islay single malt scotch (use Laphroaig 10)
> ⅔ oz. lemon juice
> ⅔ oz. honey syrup
> piece of candied ginger, to garnish

Combine liquid ingredients in a shaker with ice. Shake and strain into a chilled old-fashioned glass with a large chunk of ice inside. Garnish the rim of the glass with the piece of candied ginger.

**Pink Almond**—Get out your amaretto, crème de noyaux, and kirsch for this unusual liquor sour that is stupifyingly strong and extremely satisfying.

> 2 oz. blended whiskey
> 1 oz. amaretto
> ½ oz. crème de noyaux
> ½ oz. kirschwasser
> 1 oz. lemon juice
> lemon slice, to garnish

Combine all liquid ingredients in a shaker with ice. Shake and pour into a chilled sour glass. Garnish with the lemon slice.

**Pisco Sour**—Perhaps the trendiest of all sour recipes, this attractive cocktail sports a pretty flourish of color from Angostura bitters used as a garnish more than a bittering agent.

> 2 oz. pisco
> ½ oz. lemon or lime juice (or a combo of both)
> ½ oz. simple syrup
> ½ egg white
> several dashes of Angostura bitters, to garnish

Combine all ingredients except bitters in a shaker with ice. Shake to chill, then remove ice and shake to aerate. Pour into a chilled sour glass or coupe. Dash bitters on top in a decorative pattern. (Note: it is not necessary to use a whole egg white for this light-tasting cocktail, but discarding the rest of the egg is wasteful. I recommend using a whole egg white and doubling the recipe so you and a friend can enjoy the same cocktail.)

**Polynesian Sour**—A pink rum sour just feels more tropical. The addition of guava nectar also makes for a lovely pink presentation. This cocktail is sweet, relying only on the guava to balance the citrus. A sour glass is recommended because guava nectar tends to separate and float above the ice, but when served neat it remains incorporated.

> 2 oz. light (lightly aged) rum
> ½ oz. lemon juice
> ½ oz. orange juice
> ½ oz. guava nectar

Combine all ingredients in a shaker with ice. Shake and strain into a chilled sour glass.

**Scotch Holiday Sour**—Break this out during the holiday season when a rich sour is called for. Cherry Heering makes every cocktail it is in feel like a special occasion.

> **2 oz. scotch**
> **1 oz. Cherry Heering**
> **1 oz. lemon juice**
> **½ oz. Italian (sweet) vermouth**
> **granulated sugar, to rim**
> **lemon slice, to garnish**

Rim a sour glass with sugar by rubbing it with the lemon slice and dipping it in a saucer of white sugar. Combine all other ingredients in a shaker with ice. Shake, strain, and garnish with a lemon slice.

**Strega Sour**—A little Strega goes a long way. It is strong and very herbal, giving the drink an unfamiliar flavor for most drinkers. An ounce of Strega also shows off its sweetness, balancing the lemon juice perfectly.

> **2 oz. gin**
> **1 oz. Strega**
> **1 oz. lemon juice**
> **lemon slice, to garnish**

Combine liquid ingredients in a shaker with ice. Shake and strain into a chilled sour glass. Garnish with the lemon slice.

**Twin Hills**—I've heard that this cocktail was named after a golf club, which stands to reason. Sporting clubs were a relaxed environment where cocktails quickly gained acceptance and even helped promote the club as the recipes spread. This one is served long for enjoying after the 18th hole.

> 2 oz. bourbon
> ½ oz. Bénédictine
> ½ oz. lemon juice
> ½ oz. lime juice
> 1 tsp. simple syrup
> lemon and lime wheels, to garnish

Combine all ingredients except fruit wheels in a shaker with ice. Shake and strain over new ice in a highball glass. Garnish with lemon and lime wheels shoved vertically below the surface of the liquid.

**Waterbury Cocktail**—Waterbury is a grand, elegant egg cocktail that hits all the right notes. Think of it as a sour served at a 5-star hotel. When done correctly, the drink has a warm beige color topped with frothy white foam.

> 2 oz. brandy
> 1 oz. lime juice
> 1 tsp. grenadine
> 1 tsp. simple syrup
> 1 egg white

Combine all ingredients in a shaker with ice. Shake to chill, then strain out ice and re-shake to add foam. Pour into a chilled sour glass.

# My Sour Recipe

_____

_____

_____

_____

_____

_____

_____

_____

_____

# Sidecars

## Sidecar Master Recipe

The trick to making the perfect sidecar often comes down to the
balance of citrus juice to sweet liqueur.

> 1 ½ oz. brandy or cognac
> ¾ oz. curaçao or triple sec (use Cointreau)
> ½ oz. lemon juice

Combine all ingredients in a shaker with ice. Shake and double strain
into a chilled cocktail glass.

## Modifications

It goes without saying that a sidecar can be made with just about
any spirit from gin and rum to pear brandy and kirschwasser. A new
drinker who finds brandies to be too rich will appreciate the Aviation,
while brandy lovers will probably gravitate to silkier cognacs in their
sidecars. Try upping the amount of triple sec for a sweeter version.
Remember that while Grand Marnier is a richer substitute for triple
sec, it isn't actually sweeter, so you can't rely on it alone to balance the
half ounce of lemon juice.

## "The Wonderful World of Liqueurs"

Sidecars and their kin usually take on French appellations because most of the liqueurs like triple sec were French innovations during the latter half of the nineteenth century. These spirits became associated with Parisian café life which continued to thrive during America's years under Prohibition, so the French names are rightly theirs. A liqueur is drier and generally stronger (about 40 percent alcohol) than the sweeter crème (as in crème de menthe), but there are some exceptions.

With all the different liqueurs, from Grand Marnier to Luxardo Maraschino, this category, above all others, tends to put a strain on your bar budget. Most of the proprietary spirits like Chartreuse and Chambord are more expensive than basic crèmes. Home bartenders who fall for the seductive sidecar and its variations find themselves saving up for coveted liqueurs as well as having to expand their bar shelving as their collection grows.

A good tip for building your collection of these liqueurs is to only buy expensive liqueurs when they are absolutely necessary to making the cocktails you enjoy (see section on stocking your bar). Cutting corners and getting a knock-off Grand Marnier or St-Germain will lessen the quality of your drink for only a small savings. Instead, use more bargain-brand gin and brandies as your cocktail base; it's the liqueurs that make these cocktails fabulous, so don't skimp where flavor is concerned. Your guests will appreciate your drinks that much more, and you'll never be disappointed with your recipe if you get the best ingredients.

**Aviation**—This may be the quintessence of the pre-prohibition style of cocktail with all of its modern trappings, from the name to its flashy violet color. Crème de violette and maraschino liqueur make an amazingly floral pairing that is unforgettable.

> 2 oz. gin
> ½ oz. Luxardo Maraschino liqueur
> ¼ oz. crème de violette
> ¾ oz. lemon juice
> maraschino cherry and lemon twist, to garnish

Combine liquid ingredients in a shaker with ice. Shake and strain into a chilled cocktail glass. Garnish with cherry and twist.

**Batteaux Mouches**—I picture someone sipping this cocktail while taking lunch on one of those cute river boats in Paris. Lillet Blanc is the famous French apéritif made from white Bordeaux wine, bitter north African orange peels, as well as herbs and spices. It is a very French version of a sidecar.

> 1½ oz. cognac
> ½ oz. Lillet Blanc
> ½ oz. lemon juice
> 1 tsp. simple syrup
> ½ oz. (white) curaçao

Combine all ingredients in a shaker with ice. Shake and strain into a chilled cocktail glass.

**Chatham Cocktail**—If you have a bottle of Domaine de Canton ginger liqueur, this is the cocktail where it really shines. Candied ginger makes an excellent garnish and can be chewed while sipping to increase the spicy warm flavor. (Hint for garnish: it helps to cut a notch into the ginger piece to give it a way to hold onto the lip of the glass.

> 2 oz. gin
> ½ oz. ginger brandy (Domaine de Canton recommended)
> ½ oz. lemon juice
> 1 tsp. sugar
> Piece of ginger candy, as garnish

In a shaker, add lemon juice and sugar and stir until sugar is mostly dissolved. Add gin, ginger brandy, and ice and shake. Double strain into a chilled cocktail glass. Garnish with candied ginger.

**Corpse Reviver 2**—A hangover cure designed to help you revive after a night of gin and liqueur drinks like the Aviation.

> ¾ oz. gin
> ¾ oz. Lillet Blanc
> ¾ oz. triple sec (like Cointreau)
> ¾ oz. lemon juice
> Absinthe, to rinse

Rinse a coupe glass with absinthe and pour out what's left. Combine the remaining ingredients in a shaker with ice. Shake and strain into the coupe.

**Cosmopolitan**—The cosmopolitan or cosmo exploded in the New York bar scene in the 1980s. Sometimes referred to as a cosmopolitan martini, it bears no resemblance to an actual martini made with vermouth. In actuality, it is a vodka sidecar with lime and cranberry juice. The trick is to use only a few drops of lime juice so that the triple sec can balance the tartness. Then shake the cocktail—never stir—and double strain it to remove chunks of ice.

> 2 oz. vodka
> 1 oz. triple sec
> ½ oz. cranberry juice
> small lime wedge, to garnish

Combine ingredients in a shaker with ice. Shake vigorously and double strain into a chilled cocktail glass. Lightly squeeze the lime wedge over the drink and then use it as a garnish.

**Deauville**—Named after a French seaside resort in the Normandy region, this sidecar slips in a little bit of brandy made from Normandy cider—calvados.

> 1½ oz. brandy
> 1 oz. apple brandy (Calvados is recommended but not a requirement)
> ½ oz. lemon juice
> ½ oz. Cointreau

Combine all ingredients in a shaker with ice. Shake and double strain into a chilled cocktail glass.

**French Martini**—Just so we are clear, this isn't a martini, which is why it is in this section and not the one on martinis. The confusion must come from it being a vodka drink in a cocktail (martini) glass. This sweet and fruity cocktail uses pineapple juice and Chambord black raspberry liqueur for an unforgettable flavor. Pineapple juice has the added benefit of producing froth when shaken, so it looks like a pink sour.

> 2 oz. vodka
> ½ oz. Chambord
> ¾ oz. pineapple juice

Combine all ingredients in a shaker with ice. Shake and strain into a chilled cocktail glass.

**Golfe-Juan**—Another French seaside resort on the Côte d'Azur gets a mention in this cocktail. Here maraschino liqueur, cognac, and kirschwasser make for a pan-European drinking experience.

> 1½ oz. brandy or cognac
> ½ oz. Luxardo Maraschino liqueur
> 1 oz. pineapple juice
> ½ oz. lemon juice
> 1 tsp. kirschwasser, to float

Combine all ingredients except for kirsch in a shaker with ice. Shake and strain into a chilled cocktail glass. Use a bar spoon to float the kirsch on top of the drink.

## "What the Kirsch?"

Kirschwasser and kirsch are interchangeable terms for the central European spirit distilled from fermented black cherry juice. It is essentially a black cherry brandy, clear in color and a little woody in taste like grappa. Real kirsch is 80 proof or higher, and some flaming cake recipes put it to use to ignite on top of a dessert.

Kirsch is necessarily expensive. It is made from cherry cider; as much as thirty pounds of cherries go into the making of a single bottle. Be wary of a kirsch under twenty dollars a bottle with a proof under 20. These are sweet liqueurs made for cooking and not cocktail mixing.

**Grand Occasion**—Cocktails with grand in the name are a tip of the hat to the French orange flavored cognac liqueur. The addition of crème de cacao makes for a more sumptuous dessert drink.

> 2 oz. light rum
> ½ oz. Grand Marnier
> ½ oz. (white) crème de cacao
> ½ oz. lemon juice

Combine all ingredients in a shaker with ice. Shake and strain into a chilled cocktail glass.

**Morning Cocktail**—This hangover cure features Pernod, a sweetened absinthe substitute liqueur with all the green hue and bitter anise flavor of the real stuff.

> 2 oz. brandy or cognac
> 1 oz. French (dry) vermouth
> 1 tsp. (white) curaçao
> 1 tsp. Luxardo Maraschino liqueur
> 1 tsp. Pernod
> 3–5 dashes orange bitters
> maraschino cherry, to garnish

Combine all ingredients except maraschino cherry in a shaker with ice. Shake and strain into a chilled cocktail glass. Garnish with maraschino cherry.

**Morning Dip**—Not as much a hangover cure as a restorative for alcoholics. This drink goes for a less tart version of a sidecar with spicy notes from Puerto Rican rum and falernum.

> 1½ oz. Puerto Rican gold rum (use Ron del Barrilito)
> 1 tsp. Luxardo Maraschino liqueur
> 1 tsp. orange juice
> 1 tsp. falernum or simple syrup

Combine all ingredients in a shaker with ice. Shake and strain into a chilled cocktail glass.

**Napoleon's Sidecar**—Napoleon gets his name on several cognac drinks, but this recipe also includes his namesake orange liqueur, Mandarine Napoléon. The exotic oranges make it a softer fruit flavor than triple sec without adding as much heaviness as Grand Marnier.

> 1½ oz. cognac
> 1 oz. Mandarine Napoléon
> 1 oz. lemon juice
> 1 tsp. simple syrup
> granulated sugar, to rim
> lemon slice, to garnish

Rim a coup or cocktail glass with sugar by rubbing it with the lemon slice and dipping it in a saucer of white sugar. Combine all liquid ingredients in a shaker with ice. Shake and strain into the glass and garnish with a lemon slice.

**Pendennis Club**—This cocktail is named after the gentleman's club in Louisville, Kentucky. You'd think it would be a bourbon cocktail based on its location, but gin was the primary base ingredient for cocktails at the time and bourbon was not as popular in elite crowds. This cocktail straddles the line between sweet and tart with a pink color owing to the generous dashes of Peychaud's bitters.

> 2 oz. London dry gin
> 1 oz. apricot flavored brandy
> 1 oz. lime juice
> 1 tsp. sugar syrup
> 3–5 dashes Peychaud's bitters

Combine all ingredients in a shaker with ice. Shake and double strain into a chilled cocktail glass.

**Philly Flyer**—This is the Philadelphia version of the Aviation. It most likely was invented in the prohibition years when proprietary liqueurs like crème de violette couldn't be imported from France, but an inexpensive and purple-colored liqueur could easily be made by flavoring it with black currants.

> 2 oz. gin
> ⅓ oz. Luxardo Maraschino liqueur
> ¼ oz. crème de cassis
> ½ oz. lemon juice

Combine all ingredients in a shaker with ice. Shake and double strain into a chilled cocktail glass.

**Polish Sidecar**—Blackberry flavored brandy makes for a fun and fruity variation on the classic sidecar. Poland is known for its Jezynowka blackberry brandy, which perhaps explains the name.

> 2 oz. gin
> 1 oz. blackberry flavored brandy
> 1 oz. lemon juice
> fresh blackberries, to garnish

Combine all ingredients except berries in a shaker or blender with ice. Shake or blend and pour into a sour glass or wine goblet. Garnish with blackberries on a cocktail pick.

**Red Rover**—Sloe gin is a sweet and tangy gin infused with sloe berries. Most sloe gins are similar to flavored brandies, loaded with sugar and full of artificial flavors and colors. The brilliant red color and the fruity gin and bourbon flavor are a great way to change up your sidecar routine.

> 1½ oz. bourbon
> ½ oz. sloe gin
> ½ oz. lemon juice
> 1 tsp. simple syrup
> lemon slice and peach slice, to garnish

Combine liquid ingredients in a shaker with ice. Shake and strain into a chilled cocktail glass. Garnish with fruit slices.

**Rocky River Cocktail**—This is a dainty portion of a sidecar that is wonderfully balanced and summery. Rye gives the sweet and sour flavors more traction for a longer finish.

> 1 oz. rye
> 1 oz. apricot brandy
> 1 tsp. lemon juice
> simple syrup, to taste
> maraschino cherry, to garnish

Combine liquid ingredients in a shaker with ice. Shake and strain into a chilled cocktail glass. Garnish with the maraschino cherry.

**The Last Word**—I prefer to think of this cocktail as a showstopper in terms of flavor, rather than a rude comeback. Green Chartreuse and maraschino liqueur combine to give your taste buds a wild and constantly changing flavor experience.

¾ oz. green Chartreuse
¾ oz. gin
¾ oz. Luxardo Maraschino liqueur
¾ oz. lime juice
maraschino cherry, to garnish

Combine ingredients in a shaker with cracked ice. Shake well and strain into a chilled cocktail glass. Spear the cherry on a cocktail pick and garnish.

## My Sidecar Recipe

_____

_____

_____

_____

_____

_____

_____

_____

# APPENDIX:
# SUGAR SYRUPS
# & INFUSIONS

Making your own syrups and infusions is a great way to expand the versatility of your bar and preserve the flavor of ingredients. Homemade syrups taste fresher and more like real fruit than corn syrup-based products that are mass produced for restaurant bars. The recipes I've included in this appendix are easy to make with common kitchen staples and tools.

**Simple Syrup**—The name says it all. This is your basic bar syrup for sweetening sour drinks. For this reason, I like to keep jar of simple syrup handy at all times. Simple syrup is a mixture of sugar dissolved in water that is thick, sweet, and clear. White sugar is the best for making a clear syrup with no cooking necessary. For example:

> 2 cups of hot water
> 2 cups of fine white sugar

Combine equal parts of hot water and sugar in a sealable container and shake or stir until all the sugar crystals dissolve.

**Rich Simple Syrup**—This syrup is not specified in any recipe in this book, but I am including it because it is often the preference of many drinkers, particularly in old-fashioneds. This is a cooked syrup that is thicker and causes less dilution of spirits when it is used. The benefit to rich syrup is you can use less of it and still get the same sweetening results. Use this recipe with panela or Demerara syrup for a darker, earthier cane sugar syrup for rum punches and daiquiris.

> 2 cups fine white sugar, panela sugar, or Demerara sugar
> 1 cup water

Heat mixture in a saucepan on medium heat and stir until sugar is dissolved without boiling.

**Berry Syrup**—Strawberry and raspberry syrups specified in recipes in this book can be made easily with the proportions in this recipe. Feel free, however, to experiment with other berries like black currants, blueberries, and cherries.

> 1 cup of berries
> 2 cups of fine white sugar
> 1 cup of water

Combine ingredients in a saucepan on medium heat. Mash berries with a potato ricer or fork as they warm up. Stir to dissolve sugar, but do not let the mixture boil. Allow the mixture to cool, and strain through a fine mesh strainer or cheesecloth and store in a sealable container in the refrigerator. Refrigerate and use within one to two weeks.

**Pineapple Syrup**—A tropical addition to your syrups can be used to make any cocktail seem like a vacation. It can be used as a sweetener in an old-fashioned just as easily as a flavoring for a daquiri.

> 2 cups chopped pineapple (core and leaves removed,
>    but skin is fine)
> 2 cups Demerara sugar
> 2 cups water

Combine ingredients in a saucepan on medium heat. Reduce heat to simmer and mash pineapple chunks with a potato ricer or fork while sugar dissolves completely. Remove from heat and allow to cool before straining through a fine mesh strainer or cheesecloth into a sealable container. Refrigerate and use within one to two weeks.

**Akvavit Infusion**—Some recipes in this book call for akvavit, and it is never a bad idea to have some on hand. You can make it yourself with a basic infusion of herbs, seeds, and vodka. Use a 100-proof vodka like Smirnoff 57 to get the most flavor extraction from the ingredients.

> 2 cups 100-proof vodka
> 1 tbsp. caraway seeds
> 1 tbsp. fennel seeds
> 1 tsp. whole coriander seeds
> ½ tsp. dry dill
> 1 tsp. angelica seeds or chopped birch leaves
> pinch of lemon zest

Steep the ingredients in a sealable jar for seven to ten days, and strain through a fine mesh or cheesecloth and store in a sealable bottle on your bar.

Author photo by Liz Farina Markel

# ABOUT THE AUTHOR

Nathan Wilkinson is the creator of Jollybartender.com, a home
bartender website, and is the author of over sixty Classic Cocktailist
articles for DCist. After a career as an English teacher, Nathan took
up bartending in the Washington, DC, area and learned from the
best mixologists in the industry during what became known as the
"Cocktail Revival."